Squeak Budgie!

Squeak Budgie!

John Gohorry

Smokestack Books
1 Lake Terrace, Grewelthorpe, Ripon HG4 3BU
e-mail: info@smokestack-books.co.uk
www.smokestack-books.co.uk

ISBN 9781999674267

Smokestack Books
is represented
by Inpress Ltd

Part I: A budgerigar against Brexit

I am *Pipsqueak* the Parakeet fresh out of *Paradise*,
like the men or the monkeys who visit you from afar;
call me *Hear-no-Good, See-no-Good, Tell-you-no-Lies,*
Set-your-Conscience-to-Rights-Buddy, Honest John Budgery Garr.
In *Fortune* and *Vogue* I'm described as *A Superstar*
from the A-list of beauty, discerning, wise, wholly refined;
there's no calling me *birdbrain* given my razor sharp mind.

All the girls love me, *Melopsittacus undulans,*
murmuring tender words while their beloved feeds
from the delicate, scented boughs of their bare hands
on grapes, nuts, cuttlefish, the best quality seeds;
how eagerly they open the cage door to look after my needs
with gossip and whispered scandal, every *Eve*'s daughter
bringing secrets, caresses, kisses, finger rides, bowls of clean water!

My cage is a penthouse, a palace, a parliament decked with mace,
an airy resonance chamber, well lit, with a sandpaper floor;
I listen to people's confessions while keeping a straight face,
offer advice, absolution, then fly down the corridor
to perch in *Another Place*, behind a closed door
en route to a boudoir or a *Committee Room* trimmed with velvet
that muffles the top-secret deliberations of *Cabinet*.

With *hush hush* and *tush tush* I drop beneath *Ministers'* eaves,
earwig the *Chancellor of the Exchequer* behind the scenes;
I perch on the *Defence Secretary's Trident* as argument weaves
back and forth in the endless discussion of *Ways and Means*;
you can depend on *Polychrome Pipsqueak* to spill the beans
now the *British People* have given their verdict for *Brexit*
and under the *Union Flag* sing *Rule Britannia! Patria resurrexit!*

Government policy, *Ministers* say, will always be *Very Clear,*
as they pilot the ship of state's course with its amber rudder;
there's no mutineer who will rock the boat, causing her veer
too close to refugee camps, risking compassion flood her;
what else can *Pipsqueak* do in these cruel times but shudder,
warm, well-fed and safe in his silver cage, when he sees
the hollow cheeked, desperate faces of shivering refugees?

Pipsqueak would give the fine down from the back of his neck,
pluck out his remiges and donate them if they were enough
for a warm sleeping bag or a quilt to keep winter's wreck
from the bodies of children, women and men out sleeping rough;
shame on *They are too many, they have no business here* and such stuff;
shame on all those that turned their backs, frowned,
drove away needy people, razed *Calais Camp* to the ground.

The policies of the Government set *Pipsqueak*'s nerves on edge
with their plans to *Take Charge of our Borders* and to *Reduce Immigration*;
he understands well enough that the *Tories* love privilege
and want to keep working birds in their humble station;
but since there are too few homes, schools, hospitals for the population,
Build for the many, he says, *and from Syria, Poland, Dunkirk,*
welcome anyone willing and crazy enough to come here and work!

Pipsqueak is a working bird, a listener, an *Inside Ear*,
who rejoices that *Brussels* guarantees him his worker's rights;
without *Brussels Pipsqueak* knows freedom will disappear
in a frenzy of eighteen hour days and eighteen hour nights
serving the *Toad Work* his news, gossip and soundbites.
Summons the *Toad Work* before the magistrate;
Pipsqueak works hard and he needs time to recuperate.

Who speaks on *Pipsqueak*'s behalf? Not *Hunt*, not *Grayling*,
not *Priti*, not *Doctor Fox*, not even *Justine Greening*;
now the *Right* rules the roost, *Democracy*'s pulse is failing,
and woe betide any bird who is leftward leaning!
Tautology now defrauds truth of all nuanced meaning;
where *Brexit* means *Brexit*, *What? Where? When? How?* and *Who?*
Awkward Squad members all, can squeal until they turn blue.

Shame on *Bullingdon Boris*, the frivolous, lacking-in-gravitas
aspirant looking one day to become our *Prime Minister*!
Does the *Prime Minsiter* really hope *Boris* will fall on his arse
practising ludicrous circus routines, or, equally sinister,
did she really consider a maverick fit to administer
state policy overseas when she made the appointment?
Is he masterstroke, nemesis, or merely a fly in her ointment?

And what of the lady herself, who had voted to stay,
and now leads a paperweight government dead set to leave?
Rough winds will buffet those darling buds of *May*
with no cards put down on the table and few up her sleeve.
Not holding a single ace, what can she hope to achieve?
How many tricks can she make at brag, politics, poker,
when the best card she has in her hand is *Johnson the Joker*?

Pipsqueak would vote for *Corbyn* at the next *General Election*,
were it not for the *Trotskyites* rumoured to fill *Momentum*;
his spokespersons boast of agreement, but closer inspection
shows *Superficies* set tooth and nail against *Fundamentum*,
Broad Left and *Far Left* contesting their *Argumentum*
ad nauseam, ad absurdum, never coming together
for *Polychrome Pipsqueak* or any bird of his feather.

But *Pipsqueak*, as night falls, is not one to shoulder a grudge; he
is a down-to-earth, grounded bird, not much metaphysical,
a sobersides, solemn, well-intentioned, resilient budgie
holding tight to his perch, inclined no doubt to be critical,
but capable, when the mood takes him, of waxing lyrical.
So let *Pipsqueak* take a brief holiday from censuring wrong
and serenade the *Prime Minister* with this improvised song:

The Magic Cake

For his *Exalted Mistress'* sake
(Id est Theresa Galatea sua)
Pipsqueak has baked a rich fruit cake
(quasi de sanitate et mente deturbavit)
three inches high, twelve inches wide,
(maxime propter furnum)
with raisins, currants packed inside.
(partes ex quibus opus macaronice componitur.)

Its fragrant densities conceal
(M.Stridulus coquorum praefectus est
sultanas, butter, candied peel,
(cum Ramseio, I. Oliverio, Maria, Deliaque)
eggs, walnuts, glacé cherries, flour,
(et caetera – sex ova minime, sine dubito.)
a mixture kneaded hour by hour
(Rostello pedibusque subegit Stridulus.)

with spices, brandy, nutmeg, lots
(Allegoria de patriis dissimilibus Europaeis!)
of sugar, almonds, apricots,
(O amygdala, nux egregissima!)
three spoonfuls, last, of treacle, primed
(Theriaca juxta perfidia stat anglice.)
with zest of orange, lemon rind.
(Campanularum Sancti Clementis modulatus concentus.)

He baked his cake for half the night
(Haud dormivit Stridulus.)
at just two hundred *Fahrenheit;*
(Quia ei nunquam placet Celsius.)
brought it to her for breakfast, set
(Manibus pedibusque adstabat dominae mensis!)
with due regard for etiquette,
(Urbanitatem civilitatemque prosecutus est Stridulus.)

good breeding, quality of life,
(Nihil nisi optimum apud dominam.)
with china plate, pearl-handled knife.
(Baccas ante porcos Stridulus nunquam jecit!)
Exalted Mistress in a trice
(In quo modo anas ad aquam festinat)
has cut her first substantial slice;
(assulatim substantiam rapuit.)

then to another she succumbs
(Meliores duo quam una!)
(her plate remains devoid of crumbs)
(Ubi medullae, ubi medullae meae? quaerit Stridulus.)
no offcuts drop upon the floor
(Lintolleum suum permundum manet.)
til she's consumed a dozen more.
(Sapientia satis agnoscit.)

She wields the knife with great delight
Cultellum dexteriter jucundeque maxime agitat;)
to satisfy her appetite.
(nullomodo morsicat Domina.)
Pipsqueak with deferential wing
(Mehecule! clam sibi susurrat Stridulus
just then observes the oddest thing.
(– num oculos meos credere possum?)

The cake, prepared and baked with care
(Non sine intento animo factum est popanum.)
he watched her eating, still sits there,
(Popanum super tabulam conspectandum est.)
not three parts gone, as he'd assumed,
(Putavit popanum paene e conspectu fugisse)
but whole, intact, and unconsumed
(– res facta, res intacta.)

Can it be so? Can cake defy
        (An deliramentum subivi? quaerit Stridulus)
the evidence of *Pipsqueak's* eye?
        (Testimonium non fecit probatio!)
Can sleight of hand deceive the brain
        (Magi manuum celeritas cerebrum fallit;)
and cake both exit and remain?
        (ecquis credat exire manereque idem esse?)

Or must there be both give and take
        (Popanum ipsum et tenere et edere non potes.)
surrounding such a rich fruit cake?
        (Popanum edere non est popanum dare.)
Or is it time to cut and run?
        (Popanum scindamus! cuique assulata sua!)
Pipsqueak adjourns; his song is done.
        (Terminat carmen eius, terminat hora die.)

10–30 November 2016

Part II: The impact of Demagogue Trump

There was a time, not long past, when *Pipsqueak* slept very well;
he enjoyed a sleep deep and enduring, unbroken by lorries
at four in the morning grinding their gears on the hill
towards *Sainsbury's* or *Morrisons*, and untroubled by worries
that lead so many birds nowadays to make pre-dawn forays
to bathrooms, to kitchens, to cellars, hoping to find
in something that graces a small glass, access to peace of mind.

Sleeplessness these days seems to afflict birds of all ages,
the existential corrosion psychiatrists label *Insomnia;*
but *Pipsqueak* has hitherto been free of its ravages,
sleep soundly surpassing food, money or love as his *Vincit Omnia.*
Every night without fail his prayer has been *On me a*
fully restorative helping of slumber let fall, kindly Morpheus,
and every night without fail the god has been generous.

How thankful *Pipsqueak* has been all his life for a good kip,
on the sofa, in an armchair while watching *Match of the Day*;
forty winks, a few zeds, letting the world's troubles slip
from their anchorage in his mind to drift far away
over the *Ocean of Shut-Eye* to beach in *Tranquillity Bay*
where the *Man in the Moon* watches over him and all those
who weave in their mind's eye the garlands we call *Repose.*

Twelve hours at the least *Pipsqueak* could sleep in all weathers,
his sometimes sleeping the clock round not an empty boast,
head swivelled backwards, beak tucked fast in his neck feathers,
bug-snug he'd sleep all night long on his roosting perch, warm as toast;
but a soft pillow and a laundered duvet were what most
he preferred, with a sprung mattress to set him yawning,
and then sleep to knit up *Care*'s ravelled sleeve until morning.

But *Care*, lately, has been *Pipsqueak's* regular midnight visitor
disrupting his peace of mind, pillow-pillaging, quiltquaking,
an obstinate, troublesome, braggart, sleep-robbing inquisitor,
a skyscraper billionaire whose grandiose schemes for *Making
America Great Again* have set *Budgeritopia* shaking;
it's *Hail Demagogue Trump* and *Farewell Statesman Obama*,
as policy in the *White House* degrades to pure melodrama.

With a few days still to go before his inauguration
Demagogue Trump's declared policies have caused angry feuds,
a *Great Wall* to be built to prevent *Mexican* immigration,
a *Be Suspicious of Islam* strategy that includes
Guantanamo waterboarding, and more, for *the bad dudes*,
while *Muslims* elsewhere in the world, *being Muslim*, are to be *debarred*
from setting their suitcases down in *America*'s back yard.

Climate change science, *Demagogue Trump* says, is a hoax
because gas, air and water just follow their natural courses;
Obamacare needs repealing, since it's better for folks
if health plans are funded in line with free market forces;
deporting illegal immigrants is a scheme he endorses,
undocumented *Hispanics* being flushed out and forced to go
back to *Central America*, *Puerto Rico*, *Cuba* and *Mexico*.

So much to the point of election. Now in transition,
he muddies the water somewhat, perhaps to gain traction
through minute and ambiguously-worded shifts in position,
complete shutdown on the entry of *Muslims* being eased by a fraction
and deporting illegal immigrants redrafted as action
against only *those with criminal records*. Furthermore, to save face,
his promised prosecution of *Hillary* is not now to take place.

What's *Pipsqueak* to think, now reports of computer hacking
during the *Presidential* campaign surface to set *Washington* rocking?
Moscow based, systematic, and enacted with *Putin*'s backing,
the cyberspace publication of emails is deeply shocking.
The Demagogue's friendship with *Putin* has taken a knocking
at the suggestion that, in support of him, *Kremlin* geeks
handed sensitive *Democrat* emails over to *Wikileaks*.

No-one acquainted with *Pipsqueak* would think him truly pedantic,
though disputes about meaning are often a magnet for nerds;
Pipsqueak's thoughts – philosophical, political, romantic,
have always been based on respect for the meanings of words.
Now, *Etymology* tells *Pipsqueak* that *Tweeting is for the birds*;
it's no surprise, then, for him to be finding himself all a-jitter
with *Demagogue Trump* posting his thoughts on *Twitter*.

Busy managers, back in the day, wanted their briefings
set out, double-spaced, headlines in bold, on one side of *A4*;
not for them tedious, marathon, brain-wearying leafings
through documents extending to fifteen pages or more.
Where brevity was concerned, they certainly knew the score;
If you can't write it down, they declared, *without causing paralysis,*
it's not worth me spending my time on more thoughtful analysis.

So what once had been nuance was reduced to mere bullet points;
complex thought became gesture, stripped of all complication,
the argument boiled down to its bones to conceal its joints,
motive, circumstance, *quidditas,* mode, all dropped without explanation.
For *Pipsqueak,* exactly that kind of semantic degradation
marks *Twitter,* where intelligence languishes in the gulag
of no more than seven score characters chained to a single hashtag.

What's *Pipsqueak* to do then, other than stay awake,
keep his ear close to the ground, stay away from profanity?
While *The Demagogue* blusters, *Pipsqueak* will undertake
to use tongue, beak, brain, bowels in full support of humanity.
With wit, mirth and plain speaking he'll counter insanity,
discord, privilege and division, and in the service of peace,
expose folly, deception, and falsehood, tell truth the way it is.

Pipsqueak's Lullaby

Rockabye *Pipsqueak*, safe on his perch,
(Stricte equilibrium tenet Stridulus)
Pipsqueak won't tumble although he may lurch;
(faciliter potuit acrobates esse, iste!)
whether feeling the cold or feeling the heat,
(Res levis, frigorem vel calorem subire,)
Pipsqueak will hold tight with his delicate feet.
(strenue pedibus Stridulus numquam emittit.)

Rockabye *Pipsqueak*, enjoying his ride,
(Super ramiculo sese oblectans circumagit Stridulus,)
the *Demagogue* breeze cannot blow him aside;
(Zephyrus avem non deponere potest.)
love governs his movements, as charity should,
(Caritas Melopsittaci motu imperat.)
and he's rooted in truth like an oak in the wood.
('Quercus in Veritate' emblema eius est.)

Rockabye *Pipsqueak*, swinging so high,
(Ad altitudinem coeli ortus est Stridulus
from the floor of his cage to the tip of the sky;
(ex imis profundis ad nubila sublimis;)
the *Demagogue* breeze grows from gentle to strong
(Crescit vis Meridiei; tamen carmina
but the wind cannot stifle this little bird's song.
avis parvae ventus suffocare non potest.)

Rockabye *Pipsqueak*, shaking his tail
(Gaudet cauda Striduli contra vires Euri.)
hard in the teeth of the *Demagogue* gale;
(Etiam aconito inest remedium nostrum.)
though it buffets and deafens, still there may be heard
(Quamvis pellit, quamvis obtundit ventus
the calm voice of reason, the song of a bird.
carmina avis rationisque furorem penetrant.)

The *Demagogue* storm fills the world with its rage,
(Mundus suffusus est iracum Septentrionis.)
hatred twisting the bars of the rockabye cage;
(Odium inhumanum vectes caveae torquet;
Pipsqueak, at his post, knows that kindness is right;
(Stridulus autem nuper sapientiam rescivit
neither hatred nor fear can put him to flight.
(nec metu nec odio in fugam verteri.)

Now the *Demagogue* hurricane blows itself out
(Nunc Turben turbulentus super se cadet
in a fury of certainty, fury of doubt;
(in furori veritatis, furori perfidiarum.)
though the bough must be broken, the cradle must fall,
(Quamvis fractum sit ramum, quamvis cadeat cuna,
still preserved in the debris, brave *Pipsqueak* stands tall.
in mediis redactarum stat firmiter Stridulus.)

12–30 January 2017

Part III: Parliament must have a Meaningful Vote

The *Inns* in which *Pipsqueak* studied were not *Inns of Court*,
neither *Lincoln*'s nor *Gray's Inn*, nor the *Court of Chancery*,
but *The Magpie*, *The Plume of Feathers*, *The Blackbird*, inns of that sort
where a bird with a problem to solve might find the answer he
searched elsewhere in vain for, *Lady Controversy*
bringing him long after closing time to acknowledge what truth is,
with the clear, unambiguous certainty of a score in the pub quiz.

Controversy this month has raged over pints of cider
quaffed in *The Bird in Hand*, *The Ostrich*, *The Golden Eagle*,
concerning the least worst and most certain way to provide a
way out of *Europe* that's timely, cost-effective, and legal;
Pipsqueak has looked in his mirror, and seen in that *Spiegel*
not one but two sovereignties, *House of Commons* and *Plebiscite*,
the snug of *The Phoenix* at fisticuffs over which one has the right.

Who'll pull our perches from Europe? For the past forty years
we've been part of a market that shares services, millet, grains,
a union of advantage in which all *European* birds are our peers,
until *Discontent*, scenting power, opens his beak and complains
British Birds are born free but everywhere they are in chains.
Nothing for malcontents then to don but the threadbare robes
of right-thinking, bureaucracy-hating, patriots, xenophobes.

The *Brexiteers* by and large look to the referendum
and its resultant majority voting in favour of leave;
they'll brook no impediment, codicil, corrigendum,
and warn *Mrs May* that it would be grossly naive
to suppose that delay might gain government a reprieve
from the imperative to withdraw – manifest, urgent, compelling,
the will of the people, against which there can be no rebelling.

The *Remainers*, who lost, though, consider the referendum *advisory*;
a litmus test of opinion, but ill-formed, and in no way binding;
it would be folly to leave on a mandate they label *derisory*,
and seek perches elsewhere there's at best only small hope of finding.
The will of the people, the government needs reminding,
despite patriot clamour and notwithstanding the argumentatives,
is expressed through the votes of their elected representatives.

The *High Court* has met to adjudicate in the quarrel
disuniting the kingdom, and last month reached its decision;
three judges agreed there was no basis, legal or moral,
for a reluctant *Prime Minister* not to propound her vision.
Her strategy for withdrawal, purged of all imprecision,
subjected to scrutiny, challenge, and argument
must, said their *Lordships*, be placed before *Parliament*.

Now, *Pipsqueak's* a peaceful bird, a bird that abides by the law,
a bird valuing few things more than a quiet life;
but after the *High Court* judgement, if it was not war
that had broken out, at the very least it was strife.
Though *Brexit* was said to mean *Brexit*, mistrust was rife;
true patriots, always suspecting some hidden agenda,
cried *Now Britannia is hamstrung, who if not we should defend her?*

Pro-*Brexit* newspapers howled their dissent and their outrage;
at the *Express* and the *Telegraph*, indignation ran off the scale;
Who do EU think you are? shouted *The Sun* from its front page;
Enemies of the People thundered *The Daily Mail*.
The will of the people, it blustered, *is what should prevail*
not that of three Brexit-block Judges comprising, we sense, a
known Europhile, an adviser to Blair, an openly gay ex-Olympic fencer.

With their *Lordships'* integrity, such things have nothing to do,
substantia being one thing, *accidens* quite another;
in this post-truth, post-plebiscite age, *Pipsqueak* has come to the view
that sleight-of-hand dealing is everyone's elder brother.
But no-one's above the law – not the papers, not government's *Mother*
Theresa herself, who, as a last resort,
has appealed from the *High*, to the highest, the *Supreme Court*.

Mistress Miller, at whose instigation the *High Court* had met,
came to the *Supreme Court* flanked by her bodyguards;
racial, misogynistic abuse and a death threat
could not dent her courage, beforehand or afterwards.
May the bigots who threatened her duly reap their rewards!
May exposure, shame, and imprisonment be the fate that befalls
each cowardly *Twitternet* threatmonger, all her internet trolls!

The redtops resumed their established sordid diversion,
the game known as *Bring the Judiciary into Discredit.*
To play, take a *Law Lord*, and then cast an aspersion
on his ethnicity, gender, age, education, and embed it
with all your persuasive rhetoric in the mindset
of a readership rightly mistrustful and ill at ease
with the monopoly *Privilege* holds over *Legal Expertise.*

But their *Lordships* (one *Lady* among them) are far too well-grounded
in precedent, statute and case law to be shouldered aside;
mistrust of such eminent minds, *Pipsqueak* knows, is ill-founded,
for none more discerning, impartial, experienced, qualified,
sit in the judgement seat, empowered to decide
on the basis of law alone what our laws should import
than the eleven distinguished *Judges* of the *UK Supreme Court.*

For four days their *Lordships* listened to representations,
gave arguments *pro* and *contra* a courteous grilling,
heard submissions from all four of the *UK*'s constituent nations,
from pressure groups, citizens' representatives, the reluctant, the willing,
an outpouring of argument *Pipsqueak* found strangely thrilling;
which position supporters had urged with such cogent abandon
would their *Lordships* decide in the end hadn't a leg to stand on?

On the fifth day, they adjourned, scheduled to reconvene
and deliver their judgement a few weeks into the *New Year*;
Pipsqueak does not underestimate what that judgement will mean
as he tucks into his *Christmas* cake, walnuts and ginger beer,
wondering what he can do but hold on tight and persevere.
(The question is partly rhetorical, since at this season of marvels
Pipsqueak wraps verses as presents, and sings you his carols.)

The Brexit Breakfast

How would you like your *Brexit Egg?*
(Quomodo Ovum Brexitus mavultis, Britannici?)
Shall it be poached or fried?
(Coctillatum vel frictum ovum?)
One thing is sure – rich, coping, poor,
(Certus est – quomodocumque iudicabit populus...)
the people will decide.
(...illo modo factum erit.)

A searching question presses hard;
(Dure flagitat quaestio abstrusissima)
it's *Pipsqueak*'s turn to ask it;
(Mel. Stridulus occasionem investigationis captat;)
which *Nincompoop* placed all our eggs
(Quis Stultissimus omnes ova in corbiculae
in the referendum basket?
(suffragii collocavit? Quis erat? Quis erat?)

What was the breakfast feast on which
(Quomodo a patribus nostris de ientaculo)
our politicians gambled?
(luditur alea pernox? Quomodo?)
Did they want everyone on toast?
(An omnes super panem tostum volunt? Dicite!)
And would they have us scrambled?
(An nos celeriter circumgitatos malunt? Dicite!)

Draw a blond crown on *Johnson's* egg
(Super putaminem ovi iohnsonii meta straminis pingitur)
and make him run the gauntlet
(percurrito ille in medio verberatorum)
from frying pan to naked flame
(donec de fumo in flammam fugiet)
become our *Brexit* omelette.
(ientaculum Brexitum nostrum fieri. Amen.)

Not hard, not soft, our Brexit egg
(Nec nimis nec parveelixum, Ovum Brexitus)
prepared with such ado,
(multi laboris paratum)
were better, *Galatea* says,
(melior erit apud Galateam)
served red and white and blue.
(rubeum, candidum, caeruleumque pictum esse.)

On thin-sliced sheets of wholemeal bread
(Scindete panem sanum in offulis tenuis)
spread butter, lard or marge,
(Si butyrum deest, licet super panem)
and cut out into little strips
(laridum substitutum spargere. Differentiam non gustatis.)
Gove, Cameron, Farage.
(Scindete cultello acrissimitres milites ingloriosos.)

Such eggs as never were before
(Nunquam ancilla eiusmodi ova)
dished up without a fault
(ad mensam portavit.)
season with pepper, mayonnaise,
(Mel. Stridulus ante prandiculum ova piperocum condit)
and add a pinch of salt.
(nunquam partier edere cum grano sali oblitus est. Amen!)

3–24 December 2016

Part V: A brisk trade in insults

Pipsqueak is a peaceable bird – admittedly, not a pacifist,
but not one to have a tantrum or fly into a rage;
deal *Pipsqueak* an avian insult, threaten him with a clenched fist,
and he'll show you the tender side of his downy plumage.
Gentleness above all distinguishes *Pipsqueak*'s language;
when exchanges are heated, and short tempers grow ever shorter
he'll pour the oil of kind words onto that troubled water.

Don't think for a moment that *Pipsqueak*'s an easy touch,
some spineless wimp of a bird, terrified of a nosebleed;
he can stand up for himself anywhere, giving as much
and more, weight for weight, than birds of far bigger breed;
what he's lacking in bulk *Pipsqueak* makes up for in speed,
dodging the swan's wing-rake, the ostrich's lumbering lock-out,
he can dance rings round them both and deliver a lightning knockout.

His metaphor-mangling friend says that when crunch comes to shove
you must take hold of the iron, grabbing it hard by the bull;
and before anger's heat becomes ice in your velvet glove
you should hammer it into a weapon on enmity's anvil.
Where honour's at stake, or where the question's survival,
sword, rifle, or missile, he says, guarantee you a winning streak
more sure than surrender, compromise, or turning the other cheek.

At the *Cup Final* in *Berlin*, deep into extra time,
an *Italian* defender insulted great *Zizou* of *France*
who floored his opponent with a straight-out-of pantomime
head butt to the chest, and so punished his arrogance.
He'd rather, he said afterwards, have taken his chance
with a punch in the mouth than have his sister dispraised
though the red mist come down on him and the red card be raised.

We all have our tipping point, footballer, poet, bird,
where the equable, tolerant self is rubbed raw by friction,
that tug of the shirt, that review, that coarse, insolent word
which arouses at last retributive malediction.
Anyone truly described as *a man of heart and conviction*
as *President Chirac* called *Zizou* after the game
must lose his cool sometimes for the sake of defending his name.

Yet *Solomon* tells us a soft answer turns away wrath
whereas grievous words serve only to stir up anger;
and where anger is, calm seas are whipped to a froth
of mistrust, fear and hatred that spells imminent danger
to acquaintance, friend, fellow-citizen, innocent stranger;
far better, says *Pipsqueak*, than action become extreme,
is swallow your pride, find your *Zen* calm, take a hit for the team.

So what should you do when you're confronted with snide
allegations, cheap slurs, innuendoes that leave you aghast,
fig gestures, disparagements, words that offend your pride,
and would torment your heart long after aspersion is cast?
Should you seal up your lips with *Duct tape* or *Elastoplast*?
Should you stifle resentment, decline to retaliate?
Or give vent to your wrath, and have hatred escalate?

It's better by far to stop quarrelling this side of crunch,
to extend friendship's hand, give a wide berth to fighting talk;
does anyone really want to be given a bunch
of five in the face to be shown he can walk the walk?
Better make peaceful words supersede bellow and squawk,
a language of tolerance take the place of the galling,
inflammatory rhetoric of bad-mouthing, trolling, name-calling.

Consider this move, deployed at *Luxembourg University*
two *Fridays* ago, when argument waxed hypothetical
over who should pay what to buy us out of adversity.
President Juncker proposed the following theoretical
situation, as much moral as mathematical,
an elegant, accessible paradigm of a sabotaged beano
in the cardboard executive lounge of the *Brexit* casino.

Suppose, walking up to the bar, *President Juncker* has placed
an order for three bags of crisps and twenty-eight beers
but at closing time somebody – *Pipsqueak* knows who – is disgraced
by legging it through the back door faster than you can say 'Cheers!'
With her share of the bill unpaid, the *UK* disappears
leaving twenty seven voices muttering, *Indefensible!*
How can this be? It's not possible. It's not feasible.

It can't be, and it isn't. But nonetheless, damage is done,
as is perfectly clear to politicians and budgerigars;
IDS back at home, from sheer malice, or maybe in fun,
turns anecdote on its head with a dig about buying jars.
Mr Juncker, he says, *knows more than many do about bars.*
Cue *Spreadsheet Phil* later, on *Sky News*, when, without venom, he
refers to *EU* negotiators (though not by name) as *the enemy*.

Perhaps this is just part of the general banter and nurdle,
the political counterpart of every slip-fielder's sledging,
the cutting remark that makes equanimity curdle
and self-belief, worn at the seam, reveal her frayed edging.
It's accepted that part of any game these days is alleging
your opposite number has weaknesses he can't conceal
and that you, his tormentor, publicise his *Achilles'* heel.

But when nations confront one another, armed to the hilt,
and their leaders swap personal insults, what's *Pipsqueak* to think?
Neither shows apprehension, neither displays any guilt
about bringing his country step by step close to the brink.
Who'll be the first to back down? Or the first to blink?
Barking Dog Trump in the *White House* dare show no fear,
neither dare *Rocketman Kim Jong-un*, madman of *North Korea*.

One threatens *fire and fury*, *power*, *total destruction*,
the other, *ashes and darkness*, says it will *sink Japan*
each, threatening the other with force, courts the reduction
of our flawed world to rubble and dust should the shit hit the fan.
No point raking the records in search of which first began
by thought, action, word, to give the other offence;
wrong counters wrong in endless intransigence.

There were once rules for quarrelling, clear stages of escalation,
as *Touchstone* explains to us deep in the *Forest of Arden*.
Keep matters civil and you can keep conversation
good humoured, but rude boys make attitudes harden.
Once past *Please let me rephrase that*, and *I beg your pardon*,
you're in the *Country of Conflict*, heading towards the cliff
where your last hope of survival lies with the peacemaker, *If*.

If the door's slamming shut, *if* leaves it a fraction ajar,
If the ship's going down, *if*'s a lifeboat in angry seas;
If you're stuck for detergent, *if* frees your fingers from tar,
If you're saddled with *must have*, *if* frees you from jealousies.
If rudeness offends you, *if* offers a *pretty please*;
If that's what I said, *if* tells you I never meant it.
If that's what you said, *if* says *I don't resent it.*

Now *Pipsqueak* suggests that the time for rudeness is over
trusting that while of course *fine words leave no parsnips buttered*
reawakening courtesy might reestablish *Pax Nova*
(it's hostility prospers wherever insults are uttered);
so may all who negotiate keep their agendas uncluttered,
adding their voice to this song *Pipsqueak* sings in his silver cage
free of malice, contempt, innuendo, and all bad language:

Against insults

Sticks and stones will break my bones...

You called me *Barfly*; I called you *Beerswiller, Winesoak*!
We took pleasure in swapping abuse every now and again;
You called me *Greedyguts, Chubster*; I called you *Fat Bloke*;
Parlez bien from now on, *mon ami, ou parlez rien.*

I besmirched your intelligence, speaking of you as a *Dimwit*;
We took pleasure in swapping abuse every now and again;
You said when I talked I talked nothing all day but *Bullshit;*
Parlez bien from now on, *mon ami, ou parlez rien.*

I called you a *Tortoise*, an *Ostrich*, an obstinate *Mule*;
We took pleasure in swapping abuse every now and again;
You called me a *Relic*, a *Dinosaur*, fusty old *Fool* ;
Parlez bien from now on, *mon ami, ou parlez rien.*

I called you a *Scruff* and declared you were common as *Muck;*
We took pleasure in swapping abuse every now and again;
When you called me a *Chav*, I told you to *Friar Tuck*;
Parlez bien from now on, *mon ami, ou parlez rien.*

I said you talked *Bollocks*, you called me an ill-informed *Dick*;
We took pleasure in swapping abuse every now and again;
You gave me the *Needle*, but you were the genuine *Prick*;
Parlez bien from now on, *mon ami, ou parlez rien.*

It was last *Saturday* evening that you and I came to blows;
We took pleasure in swapping abuse right there and right then;
I blacked your eye, you gave me a bloody nose;
Saying *parlez bien* from now on, *mon ami, ou parlez rien.*

There's an axe in the garage and here, in the kitchen, a blade;
and I'm tempted to take matters in hand every now and again;
and I understood yesterday when you said, 'Be very afraid.
Parlez bien from now on, *mon ami, ou parlez rien.*'

The time's come to stop calling names, settle our differences,
vow not to trade personal insults ever again;
let's bury the hatchet, shake hands, and start mending our fences;
let's show one another respect, like civilised men.

18–30 October 2017

Part IV: Article 50 triggered, then a General Election

Pipsqueak, despite his years, maintains youthful vigour
through clean living, good habits, diet and exercise;
while other birds go to seed, his trim figure
excites admiration, awe, envy even, in onlookers' eyes.
Crowds gather to watch *Melopsittacus* as he flies,
hops or bench presses the bars of his silver cage
with the grace, stamina, strength of a bird half his age.

Eagle, falcon and buzzard may soar to a greater height
but none rivals the sinuous motion of *Undulans*
ducking and weaving his way in elliptical flight
to leave kestrel, crow, seagull and sparrow mere also-rans;
Pipsqueak aloft is *avis perelegans*,
the aerial master of jigs, waltzes and reels,
the faultless performer of twists, somersaults and cartwheels.

Yet something today approaching dissatisfaction
with more or less level flight comes to motivate
Pipsqueak the self-critical bird to seek the attraction
of some new mode of flight that does more than undulate.
His aspirations are upward – by no means to levitate,
but to soar to the stratosphere, becoming a god on
high, like those peregrine falcons roosting on *Tate Modern*.

He abandons his cage, flies to the window sill,
launches himself out, not troubling to prepare;
he swoops, somersaults, pirouettes, alive to the thrill
of an extravagant dance in the warm afternoon air.
He follows his instincts, rolls over *Trafalgar Square*,
Whitehall and the river itself, until there, filling the sky,
rise the enormous, revolving spokes of the *London Eye*.

Other buildings are higher – the towers of *Canary Wharf*,
The Razor, The Walkie Talkie, The Gherkin, The Shard
look down on the *Eye* as a giant might look at a dwarf
boasting his modest height in *Goliath's* back yard.
But the *Eye*, *Pipsqueak* reckons, is better in one regard;
a skyscraper by sheer height may achieve domination
but the special gift of the *Eye* is serene rotation.

How slowly it turns, its motion barely perceptible
to men, women and children forming a queue to ride;
the capsules creep round and *Pipsqueak*, being susceptible
neither to vertigo nor agoraphobia, positions himself outside;
upwards he floats, looking down on the full tide
of human existence making its way across
the *Golden Jubilee* footbridges to and from *Charing Cross*.

He rises slowly aloft, leaving behind ground zero,
his upward trajectory taking a circular route;
he looks over to where on his column *Trafalgar's Hero*,
delighted to see him, raises his sword in salute.
By nature a garrulous bird, *Pipsqueak* is mute
with astonishment as the wheel lifts him higher and higher
past the urn topping *Sir Christopher's Monument* to the *Great Fire*.

A city resurgent, a great naval victory won,
these are the triumphs our monuments celebrate;
a thousand years hence, who'd venture comparison
between these and a budgerigar set on a plinth of slate?
Still *Pipsqueak* ascends, the wheel at a gentle rate
lifting him to his zenith below which the city sprawls;
he soars above *Big Ben*, *Tate Modern*, the dome of *St Paul's*.

Before him, a vista extends – the river unwinds
past *Greenwich* and *Guildford*, running away to the sea
at *Southend*, in *Essex*, where salt from the *North Sea* blinds
our steady gaze overseas, and *English* turns *Estuary*.
Beyond are exchanges of *Bonjour* and *Non merci*,
the existential imperative and the amorous glance,
the *Marseillaise*, *Johnny Halliday*, and the vineyards of *France*.

Now he looks towards *Europe*, sadness fills *Pipsqueak's* heart
as *Britain* creeps at a snail's pace closer to separation;
the state, fraught with dismay, is torn ever further apart
by mistrust and regret with each day of negotiation;
what does our future hold but the fragmentation
of all we rejoiced in – loss, misery and disorder,
the unattainable compromise of a soft/hard *Irish* border?

Already the fat cats are laying contingency plans
for headquarters abroad, the bankers deserting the city,
the airlines in flight, and growth in the businessman's
order book starved for want of the nitty gritty;
pro-*Brexiteers* thump their tubs about fresh opportunity
but talking it up is no antidote to a folly
that leaves *Pipsqueak* alone on his perch plunged in deep melancholy.

What has *Mrs May* done, triggering *Article Fifty*
before calling a general election and losing those thirty seats?
Shameless, hubristic, self-protecting, fundamentally shifty,
she finds a way forward, side-stepping her many defeats,
buys off her come-uppance, ignoring the bird in the street's
indignation, and outraging all decent democrats
with a billion pounds sterling paid to the *Bowler Hats*.

For a fingertip hold on power no price is too high
and the *Bowler Hats* knowing this take her to the wire,
promising, just in time for the *Queen's Speech*, confidence and supply
to preserve *Mrs May* in her frying pan out of the fire.
Two years the arrangement runs and will then expire,
or no doubt be renewed for whoever's *Prime Minister* then
to keep flying the *Brexit* flag from the front door of *Number Ten*.

What of *Boris*, our comedy statesman lately turned back-seat driver,
who responds to *Europe*'s divorce bill with a truculent *Go whistle*?
Instead of their 60 billion, will he merely offer a fiver
saying *If reason won't buy us a decent divorce, do you think this'll?*
Now the *Statistics Supremo* sends him a kneecap epistle
for repeating his claim that *Brexit* would free largesse
of £350 million a week to spend on the *NHS*.

Meanwhile, over in *Brussels*, all *M. Barnier* hears
is the steady, relentless sound of the clock ticking;
bureaucracies squabble, and opportunity disappears
in self-righteous exchanges of name-calling, posturing, nit-picking.
There are those in *Brussels* who think that a good kicking
is what *Britain* has coming, but *Pipsqueak* believes it has come,
the self-administered aftermath of a fatally flawed referendum.

On the first night of the *Proms*, *Levit* played *Beethoven's C minor*
Piano Concerto (his third) to tumultuous acclaim;
Pipsqueak, in the stalls, had never heard anything finer,
and to judge by the applause, the whole *Albert Hall* felt the same.
Cosmopolitan, eurocentric, his playing had kindled a flame,
and to remind us that *Europe* is one, soloist *Igor*
played *Variations* on *Beethoven's Ode to Joy* for his encore.

Barenboim, two nights later, conducted *Elgar's*
Symphony Number 2, and spoke afterwards
of how wrong it would be for patriot budgerigars
to think of him simply as manufacturing *English* goods.
Elgar, he said, transcends narrow neighbourhoods
of county and country, expressing what it is to be part
of that vast, still unmapped continent, the human heart.

Pipsqueak's circuit aloft now finishes where it began
as the *Eye*, uninterrupted, continues its slow rotation
and since music is what will persuade us, if anything can,
to abandon our folly and move towards integration
he breaks out in a new song that he hopes will delight the nation.
It's called *The Song of the Wheel*, or *Lest we Forget*,
Faites vos Jeux, Rien ne va plus, or *Shall we play Russian Roulette?*

The Wheel

(Non tempus perdete lusores, denarios deponete!
deponete denarios et vobis Fortuna favet!
Nec ultra, nec ultra – incipit volvere rota.)

You put your money on odd and the ball rolls even;
You put your money on black and it rolls red;
You put your money on eight and it rolls a seven;
You put your money on life and you end up dead.

(Denarios deponete, lusores; iterum feliciores, amici!
deponete denarios et vobis Fortuna favet!
Nec ultra, nec ultra – incipit volvere rota.)

You put your money on high and the ball rolls low;
You put your money on low and it rolls high;
You bet straight up and the accursed ball rolls a zero
You make a joke of your loss and the loss you make makes you cry.

(Deponete denarios, lusores; vincere perdere sequitur!
deponete denarios – et audacis Fortuna favet!
Nec ultra, nec ultra – incipit volvere rota.)

You put your money on stay but the vote in the end goes for leave;
You put your money on *Jez*, and the vote in the end falls for *May*;
You put your stake on the tiny unvisited square marked *Reprieve*;
But *Sunshine*, you've lost; today's not your lucky day.

(Sub nubibus, victi, vacuete sacculos vostros;
carpete ab humeris detritus tunicas laceras
hodie infelices vos perdisse videmus.)

You put money on staying, not expecting to make a mint
but now the game's lost wonder where did your money go?
With no shirt to your back, you find yourself suddenly skint
and walk empty handed out of the *Brexit Casino*.

18 May–21 September 2017

Part VI: Brexit Impact Assessments, authentic and otherwise

Pipsqueak is a *Connected Bird*, a *Budgerigar of the World*,
an advocate of collaboration, shared living, and joined-up thinking;
cosmopolitan, multicultural, outward-looking, he's not one to live curled
up in an ivory tower or in *Cloud Cuckooland*, calm and unblinking
while society falls apart and the ship of state's sinking;
Pipsqueak prefers engagement, involvement, to separation,
values philosophy, poetry, talk, all forms of communication.

He listens to argument, gossip, opinion, internet chatter,
reads *The Spectator*, *The Guardian*, sifts genuine news from fake;
politics these days he considers a desperate matter
where judgement is put at risk and survival's at stake.
Homer may catnap, but *Pipsqueak* stays wide awake,
with a song in his heart and a measure of verse to engage
indignation, disgust, a sharp sense of avian outrage.

The *Brexit Affliction* has limped to the end of its first phase,
a malignant *Insular Sickness* that's travelled the course
from its outbreak two summers ago to *Decision Day*'s
verdict that all's well for moving forward with our divorce.
The *EU* judges progress *sufficient* for it to endorse
a start on phase two, with the cards to be played (or replayed)
marked *Transition Arrangements*, *Bill Payments*, and *Frameworks for Trade*.

Pipsqueak had been hoping for signs of dissatisfaction,
a hiccup, a hitch, a rug pulled from under the feet
of the *Brexit Brigade* to frustrate an ill-judged transaction,
give foolishness pause for thought, perhaps even unseat
self-serving, state-plundering *Tories* and throw them out on the street.
But the *Bowler Hats* called to heel, and *Brussels*, as things looked sinister,
cut a few feet of slack to a decidedly sub-prime *Prime Minister*.

There is wriggle-room, after all, in determining what's *sufficient*
when the finish line's shrouded in *Mist* and the going gets tough;
who objects, when accord is at hand, that agreement's deficient?
and who thinks, on the verge of a handshake, it's time to play rough?
But the chickens will come home to roost soon enough,
the henhouse itself be thrown once again into disorder
when discussion returns as it must to the *Irish* border.

Hope unfulfilled lies buried deep under yesterday's snows
and nobody knows for sure where tomorrow is going;
death, taxes and rent-day apart, as every bird knows,
the future's uncertain, wrapped in a cloud of unknowing;
but *Pipsqueak* has access to sensitive instruments showing
the shape, smell, size and colour of what is about to befall;
they are – his horoscopes, maps of *Dystopia*, and a crystal ball.

Basher Davis maintained he had *fifty-eight Impact Assessments*
done in mind-numbing detail to show each minute turn and twist
shaping fisheries, retail, engineering, financial investments,
pharmaceuticals, farming, construction – a formidable list.
But when pressed to disclose them, he said, *They do not exist.*
There's no need for formal assessment. It's a self-evident fact
that a regulatory hurdle imposed will have regulatory impact.

The Basher admits to having done only *Sector Analysis*
mapping current involvement in *thirty-nine Spheres of Activity,*
but *Pipsqueak* foresees widespread economic paralysis,
low wages, high prices, a weak pound and stalled productivity.
In a dysfunctional culture powered by insensitivity
Rag's skint, *Tag*'s bankrupt, and *Bobtail*'s run out of money;
The Promised Land is a wilderness lacking both milk and honey.

Some experts back *Pipsqueak* – ex-*Chancellor, Gordon Brown,*
and *The Office for Budget Responsibility Chairman, Robert Choate,*
Treasury songsters both, economists about town,
tell us that *Brexit*, when it occurs, will strike a *Bum Note.*
Our country's decline, they suggest, will come to stick in the throat
of patriot birds everywhere, though *Gordon*, in nuanced language,
says he won't advocate a second referendum *at this stage.*

Likewise *Sadiq Khan, London's Mayor,* whom *Boris Johnson* describes
in a petulant tweet as *a puffed-up, pompous popinjay*
(he's past master at dishing out inappropriate personal jibes
to make headlines and keep his own self-advancement in play;)
(Pipsqueak adds, *What's wrong with popinjays anyway?*
To understand this, you don't have to be a clairvoyant;
some birds have dull feathers, others are more flamboyant.)

Sadiq, a *Remainer*, conceding a probable *Brexit*,
undertook to perform what *Mrs May* and *The Basher* neglected,
and exploring this *Androgyne Mollusc* took three steps to sex it,
three sets of conditions, each with its impact projected;
his published assessments confirm everything *Pipsqueak* suspected:
downturns in the economy, investment, employment, trade,
an impoverished country, lost opportunities, a whole lost decade.

Pipsqueak sharpens his beak on fresh, top-of-the range cuttlefish,
takes a cropful of stoneground, organic, prime-quality millet;
he peers into his mirror, digs into his feeding dish
and wonders how deep, and for how long, he'll be able to fill it.
What changes will *Brexit* bring to *Undulans'* billet?
What will his future be, left out in the cold?
What's to become of *Melopsittacus* when he grows old?

Encouraged of late by three *Cabinet* members resigning,
Pipsqueak swings on his perch and rattles his silver bell,
for every storm cloud, he knows, has a silver lining
and what future's in store for the rest of them, who can tell?
Bid farewell to *Fallon*, to *Green*, and bid *Priti* farewell;
the backbenches beckon when colleagues, grown hypercritical,
allege inappropriate conduct, theirs personal, hers political.

A hand on a journalist's knee, a computer loaded with porn,
unauthorised top-level talks while vacationing overseas
and the *Cabinet* left in the dark – who'd stifle a yawn
and shrug off concern faced with events like these?
Lesser things in the past have brought government to its knees;
best lance the boil, purge the air, ride out the moral kerfuffle,
rethink *Cabinet* over *Christmas*, and have a new year reshuffle.

Elsewhere, disillusionment leads independent *Chairs*
of two *Government Watchdogs* to go of their own volition;
it's too late, they conclude, to introduce running repairs
from a lame *Social Mobility* or a doomed *Infrastructure Commission.*
Society's frozen, with most people kept in submission,
and projects stagnate while the government maps out its course
through flawed notions of progress, vain hopes, to an ill-judged divorce.

And today *Pipsqueak* learns of multiple projects suspended
now liquidation's the fate of grossly-mismanaged *Carillion*;
the compressors are stilled, the *JCB* buckets upended,
and crane jibs stretch motionless over a half-built pavilion.
43,000 jobs are lost, debts come to more than £1,000,000,000,
motorways are unfinished, creditors left unpaid,
hospitals unconstructed, subcontractors betrayed.

With no bailouts in prospect, employees left to their fate,
and no chance of businesses being paid what they're owed,
what's *Pipsqueak* to do but sharpen his beak and wait?
Private Finance Initiative's no doubt reached the end of the road
but *Pipsqueak*'s at work drafting the next episode
of the tragic soap opera, flies-in-the ointment farce
he calls *Tory Bandits Uncovered*, or *Rogues in a Looking Glass.*

A moment, meanwhile, to divert imagination,
afford *Patriot Songbirds* something to celebrate,
turn briefly aside from these dark days of degeneration
and give care-saddened satire an hour to recuperate.
Black, sturdy and storm proof, who can exaggerate,
(all things considered and balancing *this* with *that*)
the *Art of the Possible's* debt to the *Bowler Hat?*

The Impact of Bowler Hats

Ten *Bowler Billycocks* propping up a wall,
ten *Bowler Billycocks* propping up a wall,
and if one *Bowler Billycock*
should accidentally fall,
there'd be nine *Bowler Billycocks*
propping up the wall.

Nine *etc...*
There'd be eight *etc...*

Eight *etc...*
There'd be seven *etc....*

Seven *etc...*
There'd be six *etc...*

Six *etc...*
There'd be five *etc...*

Five *etc...*
There'd be four *etc...*

Four *etc...*
There'd be three *etc...*

Three *etc...*
There'd be two *etc...*

Two *etc...*
There'd be one *Bowler Billycock*
propping up the wall.

One *Bowler Billycock* propping up a wall,
one *Bowler Billycock* propping up a wall,
and if that one *Bowler Billycock*
should accidentally fall
there'd be no *Bowler Billycocks*
propping up the wall.

No *Bowler Billycocks* propping up the wall,
no *Bowler Billycocks* propping up the wall,
and with no *Bowler Billycocks,*
no *Billycocks* at all,
there'd be no *Bowler Billycocks*
and the *Government* would fall.
Merda! Merda! Merda!

3–18 January 2018

Part VII: Two tapestries, Bayeux and Brexit

Pipsqueak, still in life's prime, looks back on his secondary schooling
with a mixture of gratitude, horror, delight and dread;
there was little scope in that place for fun times, frisking or fooling
given strict rules, harsh discipline, and a *Tyrannical Head*;
detentions, impositions and beatings made up his daily bread
unrelieved but by one thing *Report* spoke to testify;
his languages shine like faint stars in a cloudy sky.

Iron filings bearding a magnet, the industrial preparation of argon, he
found uninteresting and irrelevant as exports of *Nigeria*;
integration of functions for him was complete mental agony;
if the *Gods* of the *North* were dreary, those of *Egypt* were drearier.
But nothing thrilled *Pipsqueak* more, or brought him a cheerier
susurrus of pleasure in all the crammed classrooms he sat in
than the hours he spent every week learning *French*, *German* and *Latin*.

In *Latin* he learned by heart all the conjugations of *amo*,
the ablative absolute that would earn him a *qua re facta*;
the first fifty lines of *arma virumque cano*
and how there is no turning back after *alea iacta*.
He learned in good time what was meant by *virgo intacta*,
spiced his talk in the playground with *eheu!* and *immo vero!*
and retired to his cage *nocte* consoled with *Dum spiro spero*.

In *German* he relished the taste of *Schupfnudeln mit Sauerkraut*,
distinguished a *gutes Erlebnis* from a *schöne Erinnerung*;
graced *Gefühl* and *Gemüse* with the requisite medial *Umlaut*
and with case, gender, agreement made headway *ohne Behinderung*.
He read of the *Kickelhan*, scene of the *Dichterwanderung*
where *Goethe*, at one with the beautiful and the true,
spoke his mountaintop forest epiphany *Über allen Gipfeln ist Ruh'*.

His years learning *French* kept *Pipsqueak* on the *qui vive*
for false friends like *j'assiste, je prétends, je demande,* and *je ne regrette*;
instead of *The Channel,* he learned to speak of *The Sleeve,*
and when *feeling at home* said *Je suis dans mon assiette.*
He struggled with *Clair de lune* cadence, pulse, intonation, and yet
a market place stallholder once observed, on the *Ile de Ré,*
Pipsqueak, vous parlez français avec un bon accent de Marseille!

Was this the compliment it appeared, a small piece of flattery
seeing a foreign bird hard at work making conversation his goal,
or a suggestion that *Pipsqueak* in fact wrought assault and battery
on the delicate cognitive interface between *langue* and *parole*?
Better talk *Marseillais,* for certain, than *Vache espagnole,*
though his teachers taught *Pipsqueak* it would be wrong to renounce
talking *French* altogether rather than mispronounce.

So *Pipsqueak* at school listened closely to *Fernandel*
reading aloud *Alphonse Daudet's Lettres de Mon Moulin,*
sang along with *Brassens, Aznavour, Johnny Hallyday, Sacha Distel,*
got *Villon* by heart, *La Fontaine* and *La Mule sans frein.*
Pipsqueak, perruche inséparable, found *un plaisir quotidien*
reading a *dictée* back one day and then, on the next,
discussing, in best *Marseille French,* a draft *explication de texte.*

Old habits die hard. Translation, exchange, simple paraphrase,
imitation, rehearsal, all forms of transcultural immersion
foster tolerance, understanding, respect in a thousand ways.
There's less scope in debate for flat bulldog assertion
when a glance at *Larousse* might suggest a more nuanced version;
where languages meet, fresh perspectives are introduced
and nobody's mother tongue can monopolise *le mot juste.*

President and *Prime Minister* met today in a *Sandhurst* summit
to reaffirm, in these times of division, *l'entente cordiale;*
where difference exists, how better should we overcome it
than at *Parkinson's Oak,* where lunch and an *eau minerale*
with *un bon vin,* no doubt, foster the *ambiance amicale?*
And how better confirm the extent to which friendship has grown
than with improved *Calais* fencing and a promised tapestry loan?

Pipsqueak has never liked fencing, the five metre high ring of steel
topped with razor wire, cameras, floodlights, the whole box of tricks
telling refugees they've no chance in the *UK* of a roof or a square meal
and must make what they can of life out there in the sticks.
Has anything changed, *Pipsqueak* wonders, since 1066 ?
We still stand on the white cliffs, drawn up in rank and file,
to keep would-be invaders out of our sceptered isle.

But as for the tapestry, all credit to *President Macron*
for his promise to lend seventy metres of top-quality graphic;
credit too for suggesting it's time to be weaving a fresh one
to kickstart a new deal in post-*Brexit* services, culture, and traffic!
Pipsqueak, surprised, suspects he must be telepathic;
since we voted for *Brexit*, he's been hard at work on an arras
designed not to comfort but instead to warn, shock and embarrass.

It runs from the year that we joined the *Economic Community*;
(early portraits include *Roy Jenkins, Ted Heath, Monsieur Pompidou*)
down to these desperate days of forfeited opportunity,
self-interest, xenophobia, wishful thinking and ballyhoo.
Here's the *Treaty of Maastricht* inaugurating the *EU*;
here's *Thatcher* enacting her brief *No ! No ! No !* melodrama;
the fiction (was it the fiction?) of the bureaucrat's straight banana.

At the *Telegraph*'s *Brussels* desk, *Boris Johnson* concocted lies
to besmirch *Jacques Delors* and the whole *European* apparatus;
British condoms, prawn cocktail crisps, *Melton Mowbray* pork pies
under his version of *EU* regulations would all lose their legitimate status;
the gutter press, ripe for sensation, continued to bait us
with the prospect of cover-up barmaids, and (final apocalypse)
of rebranding *in Latin* our takeaway cod, plaice and chips.

The outrageous, the far-fetched, the impossible and the absurd
cut bureaucracy down to size with a smile and a chuckle,
but patriots, taking *Hyperbole* at her word,
found her comic scenarios playing out too close to the knuckle.
The sheer weight of their indignation made common sense buckle;
with cries of *We Want Our Country Back* and *Hang On To The Pound*
the *Bulldogs* broke loose, ran amok, and drove reason to ground.

When immigrants landed, the *Bulldogs* wanted to send'em
back where they came from with no thanks, and no chance of reprieve
but did *Cameron* think, when he promised a stay-or-go *Referendum*,
there was a cat in hell's chance of there being a verdict to leave?
How fatally *hubris* led him to misconceive!
If the *Vote Leave* campaign taught *Pipsqueak* just one thing, it's this:
that red double-decker in *Truro* gave *Posh Boy* his *nemesis*.

Somewhere in most people's hearts there are shreds of compassion
for the old, for the frail, for the sick, and for those in distress
and most people know proper funding is long out of fashion
for doctors and nurses at work in the *NHS*.
A shortage of nurses leaves hospital wards in a mess;
a masterstroke then to have voting for *Brexit* bespeak
for the hard-pressed *NHS* £350,000,000 a week.

How many of those on the fence saw the legerdemain
that passed over awkward distinctions between gross sums and net?
How many suspected the work of a devious brain
linking savings of any size with relief of the *NHS* debt ?
How many who voted to leave later came to regret
they did not see *Scheming Ambition* joining the dots,
the blond *Brussels Leopard* once more revealing his spots?

With a verdict for *Leave*, *Posh Boy* tendered his resignation
(*Pipsqueak*'s tapestry shows him taking the red bus out of town);
Fox, *Johnson*, *Crabb*, *Leadsom* and *May* all sought nomination
with slippery *Gove* managing *Johnson*'s bid for the crown;
but treachery showed his hand in the run-up to showdown
with *Gove* plunging his breadknife deep into *Boris*'s back;
he withdrew his support, and mounted his own attack.

But one at a time *May*'s rivals dropped out of contention
leaving her to walk unopposed into *Number Ten*;
she made *Gove* cool his heels for a year in the fifth dimension
of backbench obscurity, counting the chimes of *Big Ben*.
Pipsqueak was much amused, though he was less so when,
wanting safe hands, she appointed none other than *Boris*
to take charge of affairs at the *Foreign and Commonwealth Office*.

We're fifteen months on, and *Article 50*'s been triggered;
Divorce Day comes closer with every tick of the clock;
thirteen lost *Tory* seats have left government reconfigured
and ten *Bowler Hats* are now the new kids on the block.
Arlene and her patriots hold *Mother Theresa* in hock
while *Remainers* lack self-belief, or lack means to flex it,
and the caravan lurches on, one day at a time, towards *Brexit*.

Pipsqueak's tapestry, unfinished, many splendoured and various,
depicts all these episodes, people, places and things;
in these times of the good, of the bad, the absurd, the nefarious,
he beavers away to record what our history brings.
Shall we regain on the roundabouts half what we lose on the swings?
Can *Pipsqueak* bring daylight into a darkened room
and his small querulous voice somehow dispel the gloom?

His tapestry on show

When *Pipsqueak's* tapestry is done
where should you go to eye it?
(In quo loco tapete M.Striduli videtur?)
And where acquire a replica
should you intend to buy it?
(Et unde exemplum emere potes?)

The *Bayeux* tapestry's on show
some twenty miles from *Caen*;
(Tapete baiocense in Baiocasis videtur.)
you need not fear a goose-chase search;
the name and place are one.
(Nomen locusque ipsissimi sunt.)

Copies exist – in stone, in wood,
mosaic and *grisaille;*
Pipsqueak has seen the one in oak
carved by *Pierre Bataille.*
(M. Stridulus opus in quercu Petri Proelii vidit.
Une autre lecture de la tapisserie, a-t-il dit.)

The artist talked about his life,
his *oeuvre*, his *bon courage,*
(Son travail avait duré deux heures par jour,
sept jours par semaine, pendant huit ans.)
before the panels on display
in *Villiers Bocage.*
(C'était vendredi le 8 avril, 1994.)

He spoke of horses, hawks, and hounds,
men, armour, boats and sails;
Pipsqueak deployed as best he could
his school *French* of *Marseilles.*
(Sans ça, on n'aurait pas pu ni
comprendre l'artiste ni parler avec lui.)

The artist showed the Hastings field
where lay so many dead
and where he'd carved upon the ground
his own dissevered head.
(Dixit se interfectum esse.)

So much engagement he had felt
he knew himself a part
of all he represented, lived,
and sacrificed for art.
(Sunt lacrymae rerum....)

Pipsqueak knew then, and knows today
how much there is to lose
when work is over, shaping's done,
the darkness that ensues.
(M.Stridulus semper post carmina tristis est.)

But that's not yet. His tapestry
unfinished, waits for more
injustice, folly, dodgy deals
that *Brexit* has in store.
(Tapete M. Striduli non iam moriae plenum est.)

Pipsqueak will take the nation's pulse,
unravel, sketch and sew,
broadcast a warning from his perch
until the day we go.
(Ad ultimam diem M.Stridulus populum monebit.)

His tapestry, at last complete,
will then in print appear,
(Imprimebitur tapete M.Striduli
in autumno MMXIX.)
the self-same squalid warp and weft
you squiny over here.

Bookshops, from *Thule* to *Sennen Cove*,
Fishguard to *Lowestoft*,
will find it stocked by *Smokestack Books*,
(publisher, *Andy Croft*.)
        (Liber *M.Stiduli Carmina*
        per *Caminum Fumaeum* emebitur.)

From start to finish *Pipsqueak*'s book
will show how *Brexit* went;
        (Insulam suam Britannia tenebit;
        continentem autem perdit.)
how *Britain* won an island back
and lost a continent.

19 January–20 February 2018

Part VIII: Making fudge at Chequers

Is it true, as they say, that a budgie is what he eats?
If so, some part of *Pipsqueak* to this day is macaroon,
Turkish Delight, butterscotch, to name only three of the treats
he eased into his mouth round about four every afternoon.
Pipsqueak, not reared within range of a silver spoon,
through first-hand experience turned into a consummate judge
of aniseed allsorts, honeycomb, all kinds of fudge.

He found fudge delicious, even though it clogged up his beak,
making adolescent attempts at song often barbarous and uncouth;
a beakful of fudge would confound his best efforts to speak,
(a misfortune indeed for a bird bent on telling the truth.)
But *Pipsqueak*'s long past the first flush of insouciant youth;
he's transcended the primitive stage of mere sensual yearning
and his interest in fudge of late has become much more discerning.

The fudge that concerns him these days is an abstract confection,
a judicious admixture of buttery-sugary words;
in corporate boardrooms it's cooked up and stirred to perfection,
an omnidigestible breakfast of friable curds.
At banquets of fudge, transparency is for the birds;
it's equivocation that dominates, carefully seasoned to taste,
and to send *Honest Joe Soap* up the garden path with the kitchen waste.

All *Europe*'s aware that the *Cabinet* is divided
if not over *whether*, then over *how* the *UK* is to leave,
and with twelve months to go, it's more than high time we decided
the shape of the future relations we want to achieve;
the last thing *Mrs May* wants spoiling her hand is a frayed sleeve
when she sits down in *Brussels* next month to promote a position
set to *optimise Great Britain's interests throughout the course of transition.*

So she's summoned her senior ministers to a meeting at *Chequers*
to take part in a workshop given over to manufacturing fudge;
there's a rump of *Remainers* hamstrung by the actions of *Wreckers*
and everyone, somewhere, has to seem to be seen to budge.
Where unity's fractured, what policy needs is a nudge
to disguise disagreement, paper over the cracks,
and credit appearance with everything substance lacks.

She was planning to bring three baskets *Basher Davis* devised
to sort the *EU* rules we could keep, those we'd modify, those we'd reject,
but was stymied when, at the last moment, *Brussels* advised
that time spent in sorting their rules would be time spent to little effect.
Pipsqueak, these many months past, knew what to expect;
the *UK*, leaving the orchard, had no right to pick and choose
between which cherries were ripe, which rotten and which had a bruise.

All afternoon long they brewed fudge until dinnertime came,
Rudd, Hammond, Clark, Johnson, Gove, Davis and *Dr Fox*,
Liddington, Williamson, Bradley hell-bent on finding some frame
of words to steer policy clear of truth's treacherous rocks.
Could a disparate crew confine *Malcontent Strife* to his box,
sail the pirate ship *Tory Adventurer* free of the reef
before sweetcorn soup, cured egg yolk, short rib of *Dexter* beef?

To generate jargon, make three columns of high-sounding words,
the first two of adjectives, the other of abstract nouns;
taking one word from each column, combine them in random thirds
and soon you see nonsense afloat even as meaning drowns.
By some such chicanery, conjured through smiles and frowns
before or just after dessert, *Pipsqueak* perceives the emergence
of the elusive, crowd-pleasing phrase *ambitious managed divergence.*

It has everything *Tories* need to make horsetrading look propitious;
the cut of its jib appears radiant, firm and undamaged;
no-one baulks at objectives graced with the word *ambitious*,
no-one doubts the direction of strategies labelled *managed.*
Remainers and *Leavers* alike can find their aims garaged
under the roof of *divergence*, with no mention of *soft* or *hard*
raising the spectre of disagreement in *The Blue Buccaneer's* back yard.

Pipsqueak imagines the scene, postprandial and crepuscular,
in which *Ministers* ease back, replete after their lemon tart;
Satisfaction unbuckles, and *Rectitude*, flexing the muscular
walls of his abdomen, breaks forth a *Constituent Fart*.
But something more sinister upsets the apple cart
to deflate *Satisfaction* and give *Rectitude's* high horse a stumble;
from far off, outside the grounds, comes an ominous rumble.

No pictures drop from the wall, though the condiments shake
and small cracks in the plasterwork ceiling turn *Ministers* pale;
it's a subterranean tremor, a shudder, a mini earthquake
reaching just below magnitude 5 on the *Richter* scale.
Has the *Cabinet's* work this afternoon been to no avail?
Where's the source of the tumult that causes such perturbation
and threatens what's done for *The Good of the British Nation*?

From all over town there are whispers, rumours, reports
and the late evening news has *Shukman* and *Pienaar* confirming 'em;
it's enough to put *Tories* everywhere out of sorts,
and make all patriot birds have reservations concerning'em.
The quake's epicentre is twenty miles south-east of *Birmingham*
in the city where everyone knows when enough is enough
and *Godiva* long ago rode through packed streets in the buff.

It's no modern *Godiva*, but *Corbyn* now shaking up *Cov*;
he's set *Labour's Brexit* intentions four-square against those of the *Tories*
by declaring a new *Customs Union* is what we have need of,
a stance *Pipsqueak* supports with a loud and emphatic *Sure is!*
And what we need just as much, Jez, or even more, is
full market access for services, people, a nihil diminuendum
you just might secure if you offered a fresh referendum.

Small chance at present, as *Jez* has bumped *Owen Smith*
out of the *Shadow Cabinet* for urging this very thing.
It's a strategy *Corbyn* lacks heart to be doing with,
for what coals of fire might betraying democracy bring
down on a leader who, above everything,
respects public opinion, is ruled by and gives priority
to the clearly expressed decisions of even a small majority?

But to offer one last referendum – is it in fact to betray?
The country's far better informed than ahead of the first
and we've discovered the hazards we're facing along the way
without so far ever having confronted the worst.
Pipsqueak's mirror predicts that prosperity's bubble will burst,
but be that as it may, given *Britain* one final call,
he'll submit, as is right, to the majority verdict of all.

He began speaking of fudge, and with a bright *chanson* in praise
of that bite-sized commodity *Pipsqueak*'s outpouring ends;
whether scooped up in bags, or spread out to be nibbled from trays
fudge reconciles enemies, melts in the mouths of friends.
A choice phrase, moreover, fudging an issue, tends
to patch spleen, shady dealing, the difference of two extremes
in a wriggle-room cloak not yet coming apart at the seams.

On Fudge

When you've good reason to fear
should your writing be clear
that your public are bound to misjudge,
that you'll hit a low gear,
and support disappear,
then it's time to start cooking some fudge.

Quasi nebula obfuscatio omnia sibi contegit.

If it's perfectly plain
that you cannot maintain
sincere views without raising a grudge,
you should consider again
what results you'd obtain
by dishing out packets of fudge.

Confectio dulcissima semper obfuscatio est.

Should the burden of care
have you gasping for air
up the mountain of truth as you're trudging,
you should just be aware
there's no cause for a scare
but it's certainly time to start fudging.

Obfuscatio in extremis saepe saluberrima est.

Since your arguments spin,
your sound reasons wear thin,
and persuasion refuses to budge,
just let rhetoric in –
you'll be likely to win
and confound all objections with fudge.

Obfuscatio, obfuscatio, optima pars rhetoricae!

Up to now, it's no lie,
you've been straight as a die
kept your canvas devoid of a smudge;
but it's time now to try
to reach for the sky
and see what you can do with some fudge.

Obfuscationes, quasi scalae, honoris cupiditatem expediunt.

Opposition is lame,
contradiction is tame,
balanced argument asks for a nudge;
let a fool take the blame,
work at raising your game
and devote more time to serving up fudge.

Obfuscatio sagaciter viam intermediam proponit,
adversariosque in specie concordiae trahit.

3–27 March 2018

Part IX: Poisonings in Salisbury

Pipsqueak until now has rarely been troubled by fears
about long term survival, his chances of reaching old age;
his mirror' s reflected a steady addition of years
both within and beyond the protective bars of his cage.
No sinister omens have haunted his dreams to presage
a premature end, with a thunderbolt from the skies
bringing his downfall, his ruin, his unforeseen early demise.

Small mishaps, however, have shaken *Pipsqueak*'s sang-froid
over recent weeks, confounding his equanimity,
the little rubs, knocks and misfortunes it's hard to avoid
when a bird and his evil star come into close proximity.
And although *Pipsqueak*'s not yet been pushed to the limit, he
finds cause for concern, brooding on what might await
when mischance rides high and hazards accumulate.

On *Sunday*, his cage door sustained a defective hinge;
on *Monday*, he twisted his left foot and bruised a claw;
his shoulder, on *Tuesday*, suffered a sudden twinge;
on *Wednesday* he slipped from the back of his perch to the floor.
Inspecting his throat on *Thursday* he found it was raw;
on *Friday* a splinter lodged in the side of his beak.
His mirror cracked side to side at the end of the week.

A doctor's prescription, and several visits to *Wickes*
have brought *Pipsqueak* relief at last from this turn of events;
a new hinge, a new mirror, and various medicines fix
his sore throat, his bruises, and settle his discontents.
But something persists beyond reach of medicaments
or *DIY* hardware – an unease that's existential,
disturbing, deep-seated, corrosive and exponential.

No budgie's an island; and therefore the premature death
of a *Lewisham* burglar fatally stabbed through the heart
by his pensioner victim, or two *Russians* gasping for breath
in a *Salisbury* thoroughfare are no more and no less a part
of the same *Mortal Continent Pipsqueak*, for all his art,
can't excuse himself from; by its laws and statutes bound,
burglar, ex-spy, and *Pipsqueak* all share a common ground.

It is certain we must, but on the heels of that come suspicion
of how, who and why, led by *Doubt* in her tattered dress.
Is a burglar's shrine a neighbourhood's just prohibition?
Is the source of a nerve agent more than a probable guess?
How should *Pipsqueak* respond with a confident 'No' or a 'Yes'
when the moral strength of his judgement itself's put on trial
in a vortex of claim, counterclaim, half-truth, refutation, denial?

In a *Lewisham* street people trample the family flowers
left on railings outside the house where the burglar fell;
indignation and grief each assert their legitimate powers,
and which has the greater authority, who can tell?
Guilt circumstantial in *Salisbury* gives off its chrysanthemum smell,
not, as *Moscow* suggests, the whiff of some *Porton Down* gremlin
but closer to home, a poisoned bouquet from the *Kremlin*.

The two *Russian* victims are put in intensive care;
in a town centre cordon, troops deal with contamination.
Nerve agent analysis further suggests the affair
is a state planned execution, a bungled assassination;
Mrs May allows *Moscow* twenty-four hours for an explanation
(it's not the first time poison's carried off *Russian* ex-pats)
and when none's forthcoming, expels 23 diplomats.

Such critical incidents call for a sense of proportion;
fear and outrage combined often lead people down the wrong track.
Only *Jezza* gives voice to unpopular words of caution
reminding us how *Britain* blundered to war in *Iraq*.
We jumped to conclusions and sent our troops in to attack;
talk of a real and present danger was, let's just say, misconstruction,
Iraq, it emerged, had no weapons of mass destruction.

We should have waited back then – given *Inspector Blix*
a few days, a few weeks, to complete his investigations,
not come down on *Saddam Hussein* like a ton of bricks
but sought a fresh mandate from the *United Nations.*
A single pre-emptive strike brought terrible complications,
a global catastrophe born of a statesman's quarrel,
a bloody apocalypse, social, economic and moral.

But too late! The deed's done, and *Mrs May*'s off in search
of support for her action, stirred, but not visibly shaken.
In these times of rupture, she might have been left in the lurch,
but heads of state rally round to save our *Prime Minister*'s bacon.
Trump, *Macron* and *Merkel* all back the decision she's taken;
from *Berlin*, *Paris*, *Washington* no endorsement is lacking,
and all across *Europe*, *Russian Diplomats* are sent packing.

Mother Russia, meanwhile, doesn't simply sit back and await
the return of her overseas agents who've been shown the door;
in *Moscow*, the name of the game is *Retaliate*!
and her own diplomatic expulsions resurrect the *Cold War*.
How long will it take for *East/West* relations to thaw?
Six months ago *Presidents Putin* and *Trump* were friends
but who can now tell when the *Siberian* winter ends?

One incident frames another, the next frames the next,
in a chain of responses that starts with retaliation,
then shifts as relations become more and more vexed
and motives grow dark as they stretch to intimidation.
A tit-for-tat process becomes one of escalation,
and jaw-jaw diplomacy, tired of running its course,
calls in its favours, turns tail, and gives way to force.

So when chlorine is used in *Syria* only two weeks later
on *Assad*'s opponents, *Britain*, *France* and the *USA*
launch cruise missile attacks against the perpetrator
(*Russia*'s warned in advance to be elsewhere on *Judgement Day*).
Assad's stockpile of chemical weapons is blown away;
shockwaves of destruction show how the tables are turned
and in *Damascus* itself, maybe, a lesson's been learned.

Sending diplomats home and bombing a chlorine dump
show *Mrs May* upright, proactive, determined and strong,
but even if you claim after *Salisbury* she owed *President Trump*
prompt support in return, two rights may amount to a wrong.
And *Pipsqueak,* without wishing to make a song
and dance of his indignation, can't pretend he's content
with her firing off missiles without asking *Parliament.*

In political matters *Pipsqueak*'s always been a fast learner
quick to spot sleight of hand, smoke, mirrors, and subtle distraction
but nobody's put *Project Brexit* on the back burner
or let it die the slow death it merits for want of traction;
in the *Department for Brexit* the pace hasn't eased by a fraction;
with these foreground dramas it might have been left for dead
but sheltered behind the scenes it's gone full steam ahead.

One small ray of sunshine falls on those who care more than twopence
for collateral victims of *Tory* xenophobe legislation;
is it too much to hope *Mrs May* will at last get her comeuppance
for the hostile environment she built around immigration?
The anguish endured by the *Windrush Generation*
calls for apology certainly, and more than that, compensation,
and along with both these, the *Prime Minister*'s resignation.

There'll be more of these matters next time *Melopsittacus* squeaks;
for the moment let night slip in through the bars of his cage
and *Morpheus* bring him the end-of-day respite he seeks
so he can come back tomorrow refreshed, eager, fit to engage.
He'll bring more light than heat to our selfish, retributive age,
for if *Pipsqueak* can't teach man respect for his fellow man
in these mischievous times, tell me, what birdbrain can?

On others' shoes

Consider what it's like to wear
another person's shoes;
be brave and test out how you fare
with patterns, sizes, hues.

In calceis hospiti cur non audiebis stare?

His high-end clogs, her kitten heels,
his army boots, her pumps;
from him learn how *machismo* feels,
from her, what cures the dumps.

Sapientior fieri, calceos hospiti gerere debet.

His hobnail boots, her platform soles,
draw down from off the shelf;
find empathy with others' roles,
and try them for yourself.

Nunc ocrea alium pedem tegit.

What draws *Joe Bloggs* to blood-red spats,
Madonna to elastic?
Try his *Doc Martens*, test her flats,
see both can be fantastic.

Calcei aliorum maxime placere possunt.

Slip on *The Fonz*'s winklepickers,
lace up the banker's brogues;
walk tall among the city slickers,
and tell me which are rogues.

Praejudicium semper calceos suos gerit.

Try brothel-creepers on for size,
stiletto, flip-flop, sandal;
old bias fades before your eyes,
self-certainty's a scandal.

Puta semel ut male judicas...

Step into other people's shoes
and walk along the street;
confound your prejudicial views;
see if perspectives meet.

In calceis aliorum mundum per oculos aliorum videre potes.

Find out what gives them blisters, where
they hope with every stride
that some day, they might walk on air:
see what they're like inside.

Et spes et dolores aliorum perspicebis.

Self-righteous, callous, underhand,
what have you got to lose?
Things look much different if you stand
in other people's shoes.

Calcei aliorum quasi speculum te tibi monstrant.

8–29 April 2018

Part X: Fallout from Windrush

Pipsqueak scarcely has five minutes in which to pack up his things
after that last song (his *Ninth* – he hopes it wasn't a dud)
polish mirror and toenails, rub his eyes, scratch his head, preen his wings,
when news comes of the resignation of *Amber Rudd.*
Is it *Time, Fate,* or *Mischance* that nips all our plans in the bud?
One or the other for sure has been up to her old tricks,
and *it's very clear* once again that five minutes is a long time in politics.

He'd expected weeks, months, maybe more, of the obstinate grip
that had held her in office for so long when she ought to have gone;
that the *Prime Minister* herself would be *very sure* not to let slip
a ruthless subordinate who shielded herself from having been one.
Resolute, self-excusing, her tweets blustered on and on;
her evasions, contradictions, blatant and reprehensible,
gave us a masterclass in defending the indefensible.

It's party time without doubt in the precincts of *Pipsqueak*'s cage,
time to enjoy cuttlefish, water, iodine, top quality millet;
come in and give joyful vent to your justified outrage
and if satisfaction's there too, don't be afraid to spill it.
When your cup of still water runs dry, let *Pipsqueak* refill it,
and to sweeten your recollection, let him also remind
himself, and posterity too, of just why she resigned.

The language of resignation merits the closest scrutiny
since few have the courage required, hand on heart, to confess;
self-interest, pride and a thick skin rise up in mutiny
against anyone saying, *I lied, I acknowledge my mess*'.
I admit my mistakes certainly betters *I couldn't care less*
but resignation today has become an art of deflection,
and confession's best seasoned these days with misdirection.

So even as she resigns, she continues to canvass approval
for a scrupulous ethical code in which all's done and said;
some immigrants are illegal, and of *targets for their removal*
in a *Commons Committee* she uses the word *misled.*
Self-preservation sweeps in where honesty fears to tread,
slips an adverb in edgeways, self-excusingly, furtively, fervently;
she may have misled, but did so, she says, *inadvertently.*

She misled them, moreover, she says, *during their questions on Windrush,*
pushing everyone's reason for rage to the back of the queue;
what's come beforehand's just beating about the bush,
a sandstorm, a distraction, a stage-managed ballyhoo.
Maltreatment of *Windrush* arrivals is the real howdyedo,
three thousand innocents caught in the *Home Office* lights
denied healthcare, employment, benefits, citizen's rights.

Set aside *Amber Rudd's* loudly blowing her own trumpet
a few paragraphs on in that letter of resignation;
when others self-praise, you can either like it or lump it
(So what's wrong, Pipsqueak asks, *with some modest self-celebration?)*
Set *Pipsqueak* aside, but don't swallow your indignation
at *Home Office* behaviour that's shifted from the grotesque
over the past ten years to become ruthless, *Kafkaesque.*

The *hostile environment* put in place by *Theresa May*
was where *Tory* intransigence first got this show on the road;
a xenophobe state denied people permission to stay
without documents proving they had legal right of abode;
bureaucracy ruled and a bulldog mentality showed
off its patriot teeth in the best *Home Office* fashion:
inflexible, inconsiderate, callous, without compassion.

The *Home Office* fostered a climate of raw suspicion
in which immigrants were called on to *evidence settled status*;
its officers applied all the rigours of inquisition
indifferent, they declared, *to whether you love us or hate us.*
With fresh targets to reach, the juggernaut apparatus
of *Government Policy* drove forward to widespread approval
through interview, summons, detention, enforced removal.

When *Cameron* went, and *Mrs May* became our *Prime Minister*
she handed the *Home Office* cudgels to *Amber Rudd*
whose treatment of immigrants signalled a sinister
escalation of petty state interventions carried out in cold blood;
her *compliant environment* brought others to swell the flood
of paperless residents ripe for forced embarkation:
the hard-working, elderly, tax-paying, *Empire Windrush Generation.*

They came here, mostly as children, before 1973,
and the *Immigration Act* ('71) gave them legal right to remain;
but having no documents years later left them at sea
since appeal was expensive, hope fruitless, and argument vain.
The *Home Office* war-cry was *Send them all back again!*
Hold them in Yarl's Wood, put them on aeroplanes, ships;
they claim legal entry, but can't show their landing slips.

Many thousands of legal residents experienced harassment,
among them *Sylvester, Paulette, Hubert, Renford* and *Jay*
whose *Guardian* profiles bore witness to their embarrassment
as jobs, homes, entitlements, livelihoods were whistled away.
Debt mounted, health spiralled, misery came to stay
as the prodigal state cold-shouldered and showed no pity
to fifty-year grafters who'd always paid into the kitty.

When *Commonwealth Leaders* came over to visit *The Queen,*
twelve *Caribbean Heads* asked for a *Downing* Street meeting;
they knew what the damaging fallout from *Windrush* had been
and that some of their former citizens were taking a beating.
Their representations, however, proved to be self-defeating;
not wishing to hear what the *Heads of State* had in mind,
Mrs May stood aloof, and made sure their request was declined.

All sides of the *Commons* signed up to a letter of protest,
David Lammy MP acknowledged our *national shame*;
Mrs May met the *Heads of State,* since she'd been pressed,
and *Amber* said *Sorry,* though neither one shouldered the blame.
With a hot line in place, the government tactic became
one of contrition, adjustment, appeasement, compensation, revival
of confidence, bandit fortunes, as always, of *Tory* survival.

The matter of *Windrush* landing slips surfaced again;
the *Prime Minister* spoke to the *Heads of State* sweetly and decently;
the *Home Office* shredded the slips back in 2010;
the issue arose from measures we introduced recently.
Explanations like this deserve to be aired more frequently;
their keynote is hogwash, their rationale is evasion.
Which brings *Pipsqueak* back to that letter of resignation.

She's off to the back benches, hopefully out of sight;
Diane, Bonnie, Jezza, Sadiq (and *Pipsqueak*) are vindicated.
As she herself wrote *So often British instincts are right*;
her comeuppance is welcome to those she intimidated.
Perhaps, with *Javid*, a change for the better is indicated,
a *Home Office* turned around with a new face in the field
or perhaps just another, more plausible, human shield.

On the subject of shields, *Pipsqueak* huffs his throat clear of sputum
and fettles his beak for a topical roundelay;
it's time for a few bars of song to celebrate *Scutum*
whether that of *Achilles*, or the other of *Mrs May*.
Which merits more praise it's not for *Pipsqueak* to say;
on matters like this, we must wait for the house to divide
and all things considered, let *British Instincts* decide.

On shields

Achilles' shield, at its centre, models the universe –
earth, sea, sky, tireless sun, full moon, each constellation;
Mrs May's has a cruise liner, landing slips and a *Silver Spoon*,
with *Go-Home* vans driving a crackdown on illegal immigration.

Exite, exite alieni! Be off with you now! Et manete in patriis vestris!

His shield shows two cities – one bright with wedding feasts
and dispassionate judges at work in a court of law,
the other besieged, with an ambush by *Panic* and *Strife*
on the banks of a river, where corpses lie blood-red and raw.

On her shield, one city is overrun with mad dogs,
its hospitals bursting, the stalls in its marketplace bare;
in another, fire's gutted a tower block, children are groomed,
thugs fight, sirens wail and greenhouse gas poisons the air.

Eheu! Eheu! Most certainly. Sed quid facietis, quid facietis incolae?

Ploughmen on his shield for the third time carve fallow to furrow;
field gold becomes black as the ploughs turn up arable loam;
and someone brings beakers brimming with *Thracian* wine
to the ploughmen each time a weary team turns for home.

No ploughmen on hers; instead, teams of bureaucrats
making sure *Britain's* wealth is safe-stored in cheap packing crates;
beside them stands *Great British Commodities* PLC, filling a skip
with *Justice, Goodwill* and *Compassion*, long past their sell-by dates.

Levis campanae pulsatio diem moribundum significat;
arator domum versus viam lassam non iam sedulo navigat.

On his shield it's harvest time. Reapers are cutting the corn,
bending over the stubble and binding their golden sheaves;
in vineyards young men and girls with purple-stained hands
pluck bunch after bunch of grapes from the jostling leaves.

On hers, there are fields of weeds. An enormous *East Anglian* sky
shrouds sugarbeet and potatoes, miles of unharvested crops;
asparagus, lettuces, leeks, now the *East Europeans* are gone,
must rot on the ground, never mind make their way to the shops.

Unguiculos lutulenos voluntarie tolerant Bulgaricae, Roumanicaeque.
(Melopsitt. Strid. etiam lutum non timet.)

His shield shows sheep grazing; the white-fleeced flocks in the valley,
shepherds with dogs, outhouses, sheepfolds, a prosperous farm;
elsewhere a herd of cattle, the lead bull being eaten by lions,
nine dogs and four herdsmen apprehensive, shrill, fearful of harm.

Hers shows a string of platforms densely packed with commuters
left stranded as non-stop high speed trains thunder past,
a grumble of bulldogs barking their patriot anthem
as the *Union Flag* is hauled up to the top of the mast.

Accelerant carrucae; vexilla ad imum mali tollerunt. Plaudite, plaudit omnes!

His shield, last of all, shows couples dancing, acrobats, minstrels;
round its edge, the one *River of Life* that enfolds and unites;
hers, a dark folly, with muzak, debt, cancelled hope,
a warden with keys at her waist, dowsing the lights.

Hic est Avernus, Fauste, nec illinc exemi.

1–17 May 2018

Part XI: A royal wedding

Pipsqueak's a cautious bird, a budgie not easily drawn
to roost, swing or walk to where others would have him lurch;
he finds his own way through the clamouring praise or scorn
of petitioners urging him take a right- or a left- wing perch.
Pipsqueak holds firm to the principles of no church;
no party claims from him its wealth tax of annual dues;
independent of mind, *Pipsqueak* flies, sifting the news.

Yet when *Windsor*, last weekend, summoned the world and his wife
to witness the long-heralded pageantry of a royal wedding,
some said *Pipsqueak* should get down with the larger-than-life
patriots on the pavement two nights before with his bedding,
the only way, they maintained, he could be certain of shedding
a distinct aura of kill-joy, turning festive perhaps, even skittish,
a *Union Flag* on his beak proving him proud to be *British*.

Others said *Pipsqueak* should see what lay behind the facade,
and go on to swell *Twitter* with verses of discontent;
was monarchist hype not what governed the royal charade?
and should he not therefore be making clear his dissent?
In the republic of letters could his time better be spent
than in loosing off shafts aimed at blunting the edge
of tradition, pomp, circumstance, titled wealth, privilege?

In these polarised times, it's hard not to be taking sides,
impossible, though, to bed down with the patriot crowd
for a two-second glimpse of the groom's flourished hand or the bride's;
and as for his Britishness, *Pipsqueak* somehow contrives to stay proud
despite wedding pomp, despite flag-wavers crying out loud.
And the *BBC* highlights brought *Pipsqueak* one thing to admire;
in the ice wastes of *Brexit*, a small, faint, not yet quite extinguished fire.

It gleamed in the coming together of two lives divided
by nationality, heritage, class, culture and background, the things
that conspired, and conspire, to make marriage the one-sided
reaffirmation of sameness culture-cloning so frequently brings.
This wedding showed what a sweet melody *Difference* sings
when cultures delight in forming a new connection,
love pays custom her dues, but gives her a new direction.

It gleamed in the sermon preached by the *Most Rev. Michael B. Curry*,
who took as his theme the life-changing *Power of Love*;
those who heard him or read him won't forget in a hurry
the wisdom, warmth and good humour he showed he was master of.
With fire in his heart he partook more of eagle than dove,
seeing a new world ablaze inside love's transformative prism, a
straight-talking, radical humanitarian, full of charisma.

Rhetoric without logic, someone wrote, *is just empty babbling*,
logic without rhetoric, cold, dry and unpleasing;
the rhetoric of this sermon was no vacuous gabbling,
its logic the lucid, just, patient, systematic unfreezing
of stuffy decorum, urged from now on to be seizing
its chance to put love at the centre, where it belongs,
a redemptive, transforming fire set to right all our human wrongs.

He called on us to imagine a day when love would begin its
work, making *our tired old world* a newer and happier place;
he exceeded his brief by preaching for fourteen minutes
when six, at most seven, had been his allotted space.
But wit, wisdom and humour made a convincing case
and none raised a hand to withhold him the time of day
as again and again he reminded us *love is the way*.

Pipsqueak was persuaded (he'd never been in any doubt)
that for families, nations and governments love is the force
to make happiness, peace and prosperity come about
and especially so in these days of impending divorce.
What can insularity bring us but poverty, fear and remorse
at differences lost to neglect, opportunities wasted,
the wine of life turned to vinegar before it's even been tasted?

After the sermon, a gospel choir performed *Stand by Me*,
then the couple joined hands and exchanged their marriage vows;
the receptions that followed paid some court to celebrity,
but as much to good causes supported by husband and spouse.
Self-sacrifice, public service, and sheer human courage arouse
in them, as in *Pipsqueak*, debt, gratitude, admiration,
the unsung, taken-for-granted heroes of the whole *British* nation.

And last but not least, *Pipsqueak* learned that the new bride had written
some verses to celebrate her and the groom's coming together,
so let him do the same (even though he's not quite so smitten)
showing himself and the bride in this one respect birds of a feather.
The poem will cry its occasion, regardless of whether
a bird in his silver cage or a bride on her wedding night
heeds the *Muse*'s instruction *Look in your heart and write.*

His gifts to the bride and groom

First, wisdom as old as the hills,
an ichthyosaur folded in slate,
tectonic shifts of the mind,
the surge of the Himalayas.

Aliquid veteris, quasi sapientia
sive montes surgentes ex ratione mentis.

Then the laughter of children
at play in the park or the street;
today's newspaper; snow, rain or leaves
not yet having reached the ground.

Aliquid novi, quasi stridor iuventatis
vel quicquid nunc ipsum accidit.

As many languages, next,
as you can train your tongue in;
their loan-words, their quirks of saying,
the poems composed in them.

Aliquid mutuati. Num nihil melior quam
lingua aliena, tamenetsi dum loquebatur peccamus?

Last, any of these; eye-bright,
forget-me-not, larkspur, borage,
delphinium, iris, campanula,
gentian, harebell, lavender.

Optime scitis quod significat horum florum
quidditas consociata...

22 May–8 June 2018

Part XII: Ahead of Trump's visit

Next month, *Airforce One* flies in from the *USA*
bringing *Demagogue Trump* to gladhand us *Insular Brits*;
he'll call on *The Queen* and have dinner with *Mrs May*
(the *Express* and the *Mail* will no doubt be thrilled to bits)
and *Pipsqueak*, hospitable bird, has decided it's
time for a summit, time for dissent to engage,
to take up the sandpaper, redcarpet the floor of his cage.

There'll be no ten-gun salute, no fanfares, no civic pomp
since it's not a state visit, more of a *working trip*;
and there'll be some hard talk; *Pipsqueak*'s not expecting a romp
from a gung-ho *Republican Dude* prone to shoot from the hip.
It's no time to button or proffer a stiff upper lip;
for better, for worse, *Pipsqueak* won't hesitate
to open his beak, and talk to the *President* straight.

First off, he'll ask about immigrant children in cages
at the *Mexican* border; did they really need quarantine?
It's a callous, inhuman action, and it enrages
all decent folk everywhere; *Pipsqueak* finds it obscene.
Is it right, *Pipsqueak* asks, for a president to demean
his great office of state by being so hard of heart
in *America*'s name pulling parents and children apart?

It's not true, he'll tell him, that stories of stress are phony,
a *Democrat* ploy to improve their chance of election;
it's this kind of talk that is just a load of baloney,
a *Demagogue*'s shift to realign disaffection.
It's hard-line *Republican* thought that needs redirection,
a hand reaching out in good will to help others who fall,
a gesture of friendship to breach that iniquitous wall.

It's scarcely a month since *Mad Dog* and *Rocketman* met
to talk peace in *Korea* over breakfast in *Singapore*;
the temperature's dropped, and though nothing is guaranteed yet
some effort's been made on both sides to push open a door.
Not enough has been done, but little must make way for more
and from both sides of the table what *Pipsqueak* has in his sights.
is the rapid and unequivocal guaranteeing of human rights.

No doubt the main onus falls fair-square on *Chairman Kim*,
whose totalitarian rule inflicts torture, slave labour, detention
on the disloyal, the wavering, anyone hostile to him
but *Trump*'s *Tender Age Camps* are a sinister intervention.
Contravening the *UN Rights of the Child Convention*,
they exist to foment the anguish of separation
between parent and child, to the shame of a civilised nation.

Next, *Pipsqueak* will make it clear just how much he deplores
the *USA*'s having left the *Council on Human Rights*;
can a *Commissioner*'s critical words be sufficient cause
to prolong days of torment and grief-stricken sleepless nights?
What's withdrawal for *President Trump* and his acolytes
but an '*I wash my hands*', a '*Do I care?* shrug for the weak,
a thumb to the nose, a tit-for-tat gesture of pique?

Now *July* has arrived, and the *Cabinet* is installed
in a fresh *Chequers* conclave to sort out questions of trade;
disagreement is rife, and for six months the *Government*'s stalled,
its glib, makeshift rhetorics torn between *Fudge* and *Evade*.
Can anyone halt the *Charge* of the *Brexit Brigade?*
It's two years since the referendum result volleyed and thundered;
now *Mrs May* treads the same path down which *Cameron* blundered.

Pipsqueak's intending to challenge all *USA* import tariffs
on cars, aluminium, *EU* and *UK* steel;
as the proud *Brexit* juggernaut lumbers towards the cliffs
what hope can there be unless someone arranges a deal?
If *Nissan* moves out, what damage will *Sunderland* feel?
What if furnaces close, international brokering fails,
and redundancies hit the steel-making heartlands of *Wales*?

Economies live by the *Law of Supply and Demand*
and that other intransigent principle, *Can we afford?*
and markets, like nations, must always expect to command
the respect and goodwill of their partners at home and abroad.
Trust, loyalty, compromise all bring their own reward
so each country needs to join hands with the best of the bunch
given the *One Supreme Rule*, namely, *There's no free lunch.*

Pipsqueak's sandpaper's gone, and a shaggy red carpet extends
from the floor of his cage all the way into the street;
how can he and his visitor truly aspire to be friends
when avian outrage and skyscraper arrogance meet?
But *Pipsqueak*'s not ready just yet to concede defeat;
hope glimmers, he knows, and prevails wherever is heard
the soft, thoughtful, considerate breath of the spoken word.

So it's cards on the table. There's not much in *Pipsqueak*'s hand
to match *Mrs May*'s void or call *Mr Trump's* double bluff
but still, as he waits for the *President*'s aircraft to land,
he reckons that somewhere about him he'll have just enough.
Pipsqueak doesn't throw in his hand when the going gets tough
but digs deep into indignation, braving his pain,
and with hope in his heart, once more buckles down to complain.

A report from a summit held

Pipsqueak and the *President* met for talks yesterday
and afterwards issued this six-point communiqué.

1

Both parties are proud to announce that today there occurred
the first-ever two-way exchange between human and bird.

An nulla avis respondebat quando St Francisce quaestionem posuit?

2

We do not exaggerate calling it truly groundbreaking.
It maps out a new direction the future is taking.

Exaggeratio in consuetudinem verborum praefecti stat.

3

It signals an end to one losing, another winning;
it's a quantum leap forward, a gear shift, a new beginning.

Per fenestras iacta sunt altae tabernaculae, adsunt res novae.

4

Talks featured a full and frank iteration of both parties' views;
each side came to see what it's like in the other's shoes.

Calceos alii alios commutavimus.

5

What's been agreed here, both parties must stress,
is a stable, secure platform for subsequent progress.

Gradatim progredimur quia consensitur inter pares.

6

These talks have delivered just what the doctor ordered;
a commitment to undertake further talks going forward.

Quodcumque medicus iussit, res ipsa facta est.

Their communiqué, artfully framed, leaves little to chance,
being drafted by *Pipsqueak* three or four days in advance.

Nunquam super triumphum nostrum pluvisse videri debet .

24 June–7 July 2018

Part XIII: Team Southgate and Team May

It's the end of *July*, the start of the summer recess,
when our *MPs* go back to the suburbs, the sticks and the shires
for a well-deserved break from the challenges, strains and the stress
that the *Brexit Agenda* occasions, invites, and requires.
But *Pipsqueak*, implacable bird, himself never tires
of indignant complaint, never throws up his wings and cries *Pax!*
He does not know how (and cannot afford) to relax.

The tempo subsides, though no doubt behind the scenes
the usual suspects connive, jostle, and jockey for power;
the heat-wave wears on, but the holiday ambience means
Pipsqueak has time to freshen himself in the shower.
The *Brexit Agenda* limps on towards *Zero Hour,*
old *Quarrels* beset new *Ministers* on the *Block*;
Pipsqueak squints at his mirror, fettles his beak, and takes stock.

It's been a fraught month, with a number of downs to each up,
and has *Pipsqueak* reflect on the disparate fortunes of teams;
how *England's* young lions almost brought us home the *World Cup*
while *Mrs May's Cabinet* ravelled apart at the seams.
One plagued him with nightmares, the other nourished his dreams;
but success comes to teams only by having a grip
on ethos, shared purpose, shared values, and leadership.

That there's no *I* in *team* is a *Management Platitude*
(though closer inspection suggests that there may be a *me*);
performance in teams is partly a function of attitude
and having objectives on which all the members agree.
Where *Cohesiveness* fails and *Respect* is an absentee,
Disharmony rules, conflicting *Ambitions* run rife
and *Disparagement* cuts through the *Dressing Room Air* like a knife.

Team Southgate played well, from the group stage right up to half-time
in a semi-final encounter they didn't expect to have made;
Pickford's gloves, *Kane's* boots, *Dier's* penalty kick were sublime,
and the whole team gave a masterclass in how the game should be played.
When defeat came, short of the final, *Pipsqueak*, dismayed,
felt a lump in his throat for a campaign that ran out of steam
a match and a half within sight of achieving its dream.

But *Cohesion*, *Respect*, and *Hard Work* in support both of ends
and the means to achieve them brought *England* their success;
under *Southgate*, the squad went a long way to making amends
for three dismal decades of footballing fecklessness.
And how far they may go in the future is anyone's guess;
Pipsqueak's magic mirror shows beer glasses raining foam
one day from a limitless sky in which football is coming home.

When *May's* team, on the other hand, that ragbag of pillaging *Tories*,
were summoned to *Chequers* once more to make *Brexit* fudge,
she put her plans open to view before dissident *Furies*
and waited to see who'd blink first and which faction would budge.
Whether her tactics were sound, it's hardly for *Pipsqueak* to judge,
but she'd locked up their mobiles, and furthermore said she'd deprive
dissenters of cars for the long trip back home down the drive.

No surprise then that sweetness prevailed and that peaches and cream
were the predominant flavour of all that the meeting decided;
but next day confirmed that divisions still riddled her team
and her hopes of forging some common ground were misguided.
Resignations ensued – who applauded them? *Pipsqueak* says *I did!*
Basher Davis went first, dismayed to find *Robbins* preferred,
and then *Bullingdon Boris*, declining to *polish a Turd*.

Pipsqueak was pleased to see signs of *Cabinet* instability –
could it lead *Mrs May* to rethink the whole *Brexit* stunt?
But it offered no more than selective upward mobility
as *Raab* replaced *Davis* and *Johnson* was followed by *Hunt*.
And what's *Johnson* up to? *Pipsqueak*, believes, to be blunt,
that the *Bullingdon Bruiser's* a dab hand at polishing turds;
since nothing can mask the rank effluent stench of his words.

Then the *Demagogue Wordslinger* flew in from the USA
via a combative, fractious, needlesome *Brussels* summit.
He denounced *NATO* allies too mean to be paying their way,
letting *Washington* fund *European* defence while they slum it.
Where goodwill prevailed, *Trump* managed to overcome it,
giving *Angela Merkel* a storming performance of badass
for *German* dependence on imports of *Russian* gas.

Her measured response took the hurricane out of his sails,
and both leaders later that day said how good they were feeling;
(ninety seconds spent headlining *Topics Discussed* never fails
to promote the illusion of progress and positive dealing).
But everyone knows that at bottom there is no concealing
a rough-house mentality prepared, in pursuit of its ends,
to make friends of his enemies and enemies of his friends.

So he landed at *Stansted*, embarked on a three-day tour
of protest-avoidance, dinners, golf, interviews, photographs;
posed at *Blenheim* in *Churchill's* chair, and then even before
the smoked salmon was served, committed a fistful of gaffes.
Could he really be serious or was he playing for laughs?
Was he perfectly innocent? Did he mean nothing sinister
claiming *Johnson*, his friend, would make us a *great Prime Minister*?

Did he mean what he said when *The Sun* questioned him about *Brexit*
that he'd given *Theresa* advice which she didn't take?
Did he mean what he said when he said that her strategy *wrecks it*
and that *Brussels*, not *London*, was where he'd be eating his steak?
Next day, he dismissed this sensational news as *fake*
put about by a newspaper having a fit of the grumps
although *Pipsqueak* could see all along it was coming up *Trumps*.

Mrs May and the *President*, side by side on the podium,
were proof that nowadays anything spirit'll do, flesh'll;
best friends once again, she purged the morning of odium
while he set *The Relationship* at *the highest level of special.*
But *Pipsqueak* still doubts if her vision of starting afresh'll
keep the country afloat, stop the economy running aground as
we hit *Brexit* next *March* and the *UK* finally founders.

After tea with *The Queen*, he made his way north of the border
for golf before meeting his *Russian* counterpart in *Helsinki*
where he contrived once again to promote diplomatic disorder.
Asked *Had Russia hacked his election?* without pausing to think, he
answered *Why would they?* unaware of the stink he
'd cause, giving *Vladimir Vladimirovich* a buttering
with the *F.B.I.* back at the ranch left raging and spluttering.

Next day, when outrage (and worse) hit the president's fan
he made a correction – he'd meant to say *Why would they not?*
Double negatives ghosted their fog, and fake grammar began
to condone, to excuse, (not explain) why his collar grew hot.
Pipsqueak could see *Mr Demagogue* losing the plot
as he'd done back in *London*, when *Mrs May* asked what to do
about *Brussels* and *Brexit*, and his advice was to sue.

Back in *Tweetsville* (the *White House*) no doubt he too's taken stock
of a trip that drew protests, mixed quarrel with satisfaction;
mainland *Europe* lay somewhere between a hard place and a rock
but *Theme Park UK* comprised a prime tourist attraction.
One element only, a long-publicised piece of the action,
his *Q and A session* with *Pipsqueak,* did not take place,
time-squeezed he maintains (dropped, *Pipsqueak* suspects, to save face.)

The circus rolls on. *Mrs May*'s taken personal charge
of *Brexit* negotiations ahead of *October*'s meeting
that will settle our terms of withdrawal and set us at large,
or seal once and for all the conditions of our retreating.
The *Vote Leave Campaign* has been found guilty of cheating,
Gove, Johnson, and others doing the country proud
having spent £500,000 more than electoral rules allowed.

Dominic Raab, our new *Brexit* minister, (*Mrs May*'s understudy)
has wasted no time but come storming out of his blocks;
to make *Michel Barnier* his special *EU* best buddy
he's given him a copy of *The Hedgehog and the Fox.*
It's *Isaiah Berlin*'s study of thinking outside the box
(fox cunning, fox tactic-shifts, sudden changes of protocol,
versus the one hedgehog move, slow, uninspiring, predictable.)

Raab no doubt implies we're the foxes, quick to propose
shedloads of post-*Brexit* alternatives at the drop of a hat,
while the hedgehog *EU* simply knows what it knows what it knows,
and when it's once more repeated the four guiding freedoms, that's that.
But *Pipsqueak* has read *Berlin*'s essay, and smelling a rat,
sees how easy it is to turn all *Raab* implies on its head,
reading *EU* as fox, and *UK* as hedgehog instead.

Like the hedgehog we're stuck in pursuit of a single end,
curled up in our insular ball, unprepared to rethink;
lacking lateral thought, *Hedgehog Britain*'s unable to bend,
but trundles its way ever closer towards the brink.
Bigots, liars and shysters throw all bar the kitchen sink
in the wake of an ill-judged and badly-flawed referendum
and no one is left with the will, strength and means to upendum.

If we truly were foxes, we'd have long ago broken loose
of a narrow majority voting in favour of leave
or at least taken steps, now we know who is cooking our goose,
to find out what today's much more savvy electors believe.
It should be in their power at this stage to endorse or reprieve,
but *Hedgehog Mind*, facing a challenge, maintains that what's right
is to stick with *Plan A*, make a spiky ball, and sit tight.

The essay explores whether *Tolstoy*, in *War and Peace*,
took a fox's or hedgehog's perspective on how things occurred;
it concludes he acknowledged the formative role of caprice,
the dynamics of guesswork, chance, partial ignorance, the absurd;
in the turmoil of *Borodino*, what *Tolstoy* heard
were the frantic, bewildered shouts from the *Generals*' tents,
the shrill, anguished cries of the slaughtering regiments.

So *Tolstoy* was fox, who yearned for a grand illusion,
the hedgehog conception of strategy grinding its way
towards monolithic achievement, but seeing instead confusion,
unsought, unexpected, the vectors of disarray.
And *Pipsqueak* thinks *Brexit* so far has been a display
not of purposeful thinking, but crude interpersonal quarrels,
the blundering shifts of leaders with dodgy morals.

What goes on in the street? It's not *Brexit* but making a living
that drives on and consumes the resources of *Patriot Soap*
and so thinking like foxes must be the best way of giving
Joe, *Jane*, and the children a life with some genuine hope.
There's still time before *March* to pull back from the slippery slope,
to sack hedgehogs, turn foxes, draw up fresh referenda
and put staying in *Europe* back on the *UK* agenda.

August's come, and some rain. Welcome thunderstorms bring
relief from humidity, putting an end to the drought;
could our hedgehog *Saharas* be flooded by anything
more welcome than fox-thought, more prospect-enhancing than doubt?
Let *Brexit* go *Brexit*. What *Britain* should be about
is invention, receptiveness, feeling, the heart to belong,
the burden and import, this, of all *Pipsqueak*'s song.

A song for Europe

Let *Pipsqueak* sing as well he may
of all our friends so far away,
romantic *Czechs* who take the air
in *Praha*'s King *Vaclavske* Square,
brave *Austrians* who without fear
scale dizzy heights of *Belvedere.*

♪ ♪ ♫

Join in! Join in! – should you refuse,
maudite maudite soyte bouche malheurewse!

Now let him, perched on *Berlin*'s Gate,
with *Mrs Merkel* celebrate;
sing *Riga, Lisbon* and *Sofia,*
Greek speaking *Cypriot Nicosia.*

Next let us all of *Sweden* sing
Lund, Malmö, Stockholm, Linköping.

Join in – and mind those ps and qs!
Maudite maudite soyte bouche malheurewse!

♫ ♫ ♫ ♫ ♫

And now atop the *Eiffel Tower,*
hail fleur-de-lys, fair *France*'s flower,
sing *Brussels, Zagreb,* and *Tallinn,*
Madrid, Vilnius and *Dublin.*

Let us sing *Finland, Bucharest,*
sing *Bratislava, Budapest,*
and from the high *Acropolis,*
sing *Athens,* Greeks' *Metropolis.*

Join in – what should we fear to lose?
maudite maudite soyte bouche malheurewse!

♪ ♪ ♫

Our song will be so much the better
embracing *Rome, Milan, Valletta,*
Luxemburg, Lublijana, furthermore,
København, Amsterdam, Warsaw.

Our song has all the yeast and leaven
of the *EU*'s twenty seven;
So all that can be missing then
are *Cockney Bow Bells* and *Big Ben.*

Bring *Bow Bells* and *Big Ben* along
Ding dong, ding dong, ding dong, ding dong,
ding dong, ding dong, ding dong, ding dong
in a loud peal to end our song.
Maudite maudite soyte bouche malheurewse!
Join in and make our song joyeuse!

24 July–13August 2018

Part XIV: Pre-Eurosummit manoeuvres

Since *Pipsqueak* was hatched, he's been just one card short of a deck,
lacking trickery, cunning, the skill to deceive or disguise;
come hell or high water, he's no good at putting his neck
on the line to win credit for falsehood, fibs, half-truths or packs of lies.
You can read *Pipsqueak*'s mind straightaway when you look in his eyes;
frank, fearless and forthright, *Pipsqueak* has been from his youth
clear-sighted, plain speaking, the faithful adherent of truth.

There's no misdirection from *Pipsqueak*, no smoke, mirrors, false trails,
no mealy mouthed, juggling words, the hoodwink of bluff;
when he opens his beak the clear voice of truth's what prevails;
he says what he's thinking, a word to the wise is enough.
Equivocation and palter *Pipsqueak* discards as the stuff
bad intentions are made of, the first step down the slippery slope
that leads on to misery, forfeited trust, goodwill and hope.

In *Poker School* once, he studied the rules of the game,
the sequence of flop, turn and river, the crucial importance of hush;
within a short time he could remember, distinguish and name
pairs, three of a kind, straight, full house, and running flush.
But fear (or excitement) made him turn pale (or blush)
whenever he looked in his hand and saw queen, king or ace.
Pipsqueak had no way of retaining the requisite poker face.

So perfectly truthful was *Pipsqueak* his features betrayed him;
an ace in the hole set his rock-steady eyelids a-flutter;
the table could see when a particular card had dismayed him –
wings quivered, claws twitched; other players could hear him mutter
Get a grip, Pipsqueak! Stay calm! It was pure bread and butter
playing cards against *Pipsqueak,* seeing just when to bet the flop,
when to check, call or raise, when to throw in your hand and stop.

One night, long ago, *Pipsqueak* tried hard to dissemble
(it was his first and last game of competitive *Texas Hold'em*);
as soon as he bluffed, other players could see his beak tremble
(what he held in his hand, he might just as well simply have told'em).
A voice in his ear murmured *Pipsqueak, the time's come to fold'em;
you'd do better, and have more fun, playing noughts and crosses.*
So he quit playing poker, stayed truthful, and rode out his losses.

But he's kept a keen eye ever since on the tactics of bluffers,
nowhere more so these days than on those in the *Brexit Casino*
where the stakes are so high that whoever's game hits the buffers
finds their blood pressure rising, their pulse racing *andantino.*
Bad weather from *Brussels* brings *Britain* her own special *El Nino,*
a storm of redundancies, bankruptcies, closures, foreclosures, lost trade,
as we pick up the debris of another *low* (greedy) *dishonest decade.*

With barely six weeks to go to the *EU*'s *October* summit
there's opposition to *Mrs May's* most recent *Chequers Proposal*;
the deck's stacked against her, so how should she overcome it,
given a low-ranking hand that's ill-suited for her disposal?
Lacking aces, she must play the one single card that she knows'll
both make her look strong and make her opponents squeal;
it's that sunken-cheeked, skeletal, hollow-eyed, spectral face-card, *No Deal.*

Better focus on *Goods* (leaving *Services* out of account)
better keep the free flow of traffic over the *Irish* border;
better harmonise standards, rules, regulations; better discount
EU bureaucracy, line up our ducks in good order,
hire intelligent software, chip, laser beam, data recorder;
better, surely, these *Chequers Provisions,* says *Mrs May*, (let's be candid)
than leave the *EU* next *March* with *No-Deal*, friendless and empty-handed.

But to be on the safe side, she's advising some 80+ sectors
of the *UK* economy on what forms of contingency planning
for a no-deal scenario might best protect frantic directors
beset by red tape, and (just maybe) stop businesses panning.
The doom-laden prophecies already have *Pipsqueak* scanning
supply lists to meet all the needs of his *Spartan* billet –
stockpiles of cuttlefish, water, wine, sandpaper, fortified millet.

At the same time, she says it won't be the end of the world
if we leave the *EU* with nothing – there are always alternatives;
she spends three days in *Africa* and flies back having unfurled
a small bundle of trade deals shrink-wrapped in *Tory* superlatives.
Will they pacify hard-nosed, hard-*Brexit Conservatives*?
Can a rollover pudding be all the *Prime Minister* proves
on the dance floors of *Kenya*, busting her *Maybot* moves?

On the *Eurofloor* parquet, meanwhile, *M. Barnier* shuffles
soft shoes and steel toecaps, cold shoulders and heart-warming glances;
one day he declares that the *UK* shall pick no truffles,
and next morning refers to joint hitherto unimagined advances.
It leaves *Pipsqueak* wondering whether the *Brexit* dance is
a hokey-cokey or waltz, a jitterbug stuck on repeat,
a tarantella, a limbo, or a tango for four left feet.

Where's *Pipsqueak* to turn for signs of hope, comfort's crumbs?
Labour's falling apart, torn by anti-*Semitic* dissention,
and *Conference* is likely to give a substantial thumbs
down to a policy *U-turn* that might spark a *Remain* intervention.
The *GMB*'s call for a referendum hardly merits a mention
since it's framed only to seal our divorce after *Parliament* checks it,
leaving unasked one final time the key question, *Remain or Brexit?*

Pipsqueak long ago found there was no benefit to be had
backing valueless hands and getting shut out in the cold;
only spendthrifts and madmen throw good money after bad,
bankrupting themselves in the vain pursuit of *Fools' Gold.*
The time's surely come to jack in *Project Brexit* and fold,
tell *Brussels* we'll stay, ride our losses (it's not too late)
and rebuild our lives as one of the *Twenty-Eight.*

Last night *Pipsqueak* dreamed he heard patriot voices raising
the *Albert Hall*'s roof with the words of soul-stirring song;
he couldn't be sure precisely what land they were praising
the tune was familiar, but all the lyrics were wrong.
As thousands of voices joined in the sing-along,
Pipsqueak laboured all night to sift the cream from the curds
and by daybreak had heard, caught, learned and remembered these words.

An anthem for Cuckooland	*Carmen pro patria cuculorum*
Hail to our *Wonderland* gracious *Cloud Cuckooland*, *God* save us all! From cuckoos small and great, let our song celebrate the one-nation *Cuckoo State*; on you we call!	*Salve domus cuculorum* *ubi vivant Folly's Quorum!* *ex substante somniorum* *crescat patria cuculorum!*
Nothing more *Cuckoo* spends on her abandoned friends for their joint good but gambles resources on bluffs, on divorces, obeys market forces as *Cloud Cuckoos* should!	*Nihil domus cuculorum* *propter vitas amicorum;* *solo nobis refert forum* *sancta patria cuculorum!*
May all in *Europe* cast *Envy*'s green eyes aghast at *Cuckooland*'s fame! No more may marauders cross *Cuckooland*'s borders, their knavish disorders her burden, their shame!	*Nunquam domus cuculorum* *libet vitae barbarorum!* *exite, nisi Anglicorum,* *sancta patria cuculorum!*
Set free from *Brussels*' rule *Cuckooland*'s no-one's fool; she throws off her shrouds! May *Cuckoos' Utopia* become no dystopia, her full cornucopia rain down from the clouds!	*Salve domus cuculorum!* *delecta patria deorum* *salve domus inanorum!* *felix patria cuculorum!*
May *Cuckoos' Utopia* become no dystopia ; her full cornucopia rain down from the clouds!	

16 August–10 September 2018

Part XV: Party Conference season

It's *Conference Time*, and *Pipsqueak*'s set out on a quest
to find out at this critical stage how the main parties clarify
their proposals for *Brexit*, putting their plans to the test
of debate and discussion for members to ratify
(*Yes!*), change (*It's a partly*) or throw out *(It's pie in the sky)*;
to be on the safe side should passenger services fail,
he makes his own way rather than travel by rail.

His luggage is packed (a budgie, you know, travels light)
just a pencil, a notebook, a small pack of fortified cuttle
to keep him alive, on the ball, and above all able to write
down no doubt heated exchanges of claim, counterclaim and rebuttal.
Nothing interests *Pipsqueak* more than when argument's subtle
elaborations unfold to make a conclusion plain,
Brexiteers urging we leave, *Remainers* that we remain.

So to *Manchester* first, where the *TUC Conference* votes
on a *Brexit* position still nowhere near cut and dried;
it's hard to find common ground both for sheep and for goats
where putting your heart in your mouth is a matter of pride.
Should we stay? Should we go? How can we bridge our divide?
Both *Chequers* and *No deal* open a bucket of worms;
If we're leaving there must be a people's vote on the terms.

Pipsqueak reflects on the scope, force, and implication of *If*;
its prudent ambivalence taxes his brain, makes him wince;
the pure hypothetical frequently carries a whiff
of affirmed antecedent, bearing the burden of *Since* –
as in *Sunshine, if that's what you think, you'll never convince
us to endorse any separation agreement that robs
us of workers' rights, cuts public services, and costs jobs.*

The *TUC* to its credit wants any *Brexit* egg boiled very soft,
without tariffs or barriers keeping *EU*-wide frictionless trade;
Pipsqueak honours the moral imperative shouldered aloft
though keeping faith with the referendum result leaves him dismayed;
had naked ambition not sided with lies to persuade
Joe Soap and three more in every hundred of us to vote leave
we'd have wiped *The Toff*'s nose and kept *Brexit* snot off our sleeve.

The *TUC* treats the *Brexit* referendum result with *respect*
but *Pipsqueak*'s not sure what this means at the end of the day;
with such nuanced language it's hard to know what to expect –
does it mean *we shall leave*? does it leave the door open for *stay*?
It's the same with a motion to push for a *Final Say*;
it *remains on the table* – could this signify, once again,
that the *TUC* 's prepared for the *UK* to opt for remain?

We shall see, we shall see – right now it's all up in the air
and no-one can tell what the next few tomorrows may bring;
ought *Pipsqueak* to stockpile provisions, having little to spare?
should he go cap in hand to the nearest street corner and sing?
Who'll think self-sufficiency's such a wonderful thing
when productivity fails, austerity sings the blues,
and the *M20* verge reeks with thousands of portaloos?

The *Lib Dems* meet in *Brighton*, and *Pipsqueak* is hot on the trail
of *Sir Vince* and his team, whose slogan is *Demand Better*;
if the *Lib Dems* could somehow get *Project Brexit* to fail,
Pipsqueak would be pleased to acknowledge himself their debtor.
Hope, someone said, springs eternal but it's not yet a
season for celebration while *Mrs May* disregards
a sceptical public and *Brexit* remains on the cards.

All credit then to *Sir Vince* for a combative stance –
We are solid we need to vote against Brexit and stop it –
but even though led by a man who can gracefully dance
could twelve *Lib Dem MPs* on their own force the *UK* to drop it?
How long before *Parliament* tells *Patriot Myopes* to hop it?
How long before *Zealots* wake up to the merits of caution
and the *UK* recovers her long-vanished sense of proportion?

Sir Vince says a fresh vote could be arranged *within weeks*
though he doesn't suggest what options it may propose,
and whether by then he'll have secured the retirement he seeks
and the *Lib Dems* have a fresh leader, nobody knows.
Will *Mistress Miller* take over the helm when *Sir Ca(pa)ble* goes?
She denies that she will, although *Pipsqueak* suspects there's temptation
for one moved to tears when met with a standing ovation.

It's time to move on, though not before noting a hiccup
that justifies *Pipsqueak* giving *Sir Vincent* the bird;
was it simply a *Freudian* slip, or an autocue pickup
gone haywire that led to the babblegook *Pipsqueak* heard?
Erotic is fine, and *spasm*'s by no means absurd
but *spesm*'s non-existent, and *egosotic* is jangled;
so one way and another, *Sir Vince*, your rhetoric's mangled.

Wherever you go, you should always look over your shoulder
was a principle drilled into *Pipsqueak* in primary school;
he remembers it now, little wiser though so much older,
leaving *Brighton* behind and heading for *Liverpool.*
Peripheral vision he knows is a powerful tool,
and his teachers were right, all those years ago, to insist
on his looking about him for what he'd have otherwise missed.

The *Prime Minister's* flown off to *Salzburg* and already returned
from a ten minute pitch to sell what she signed up to at *Chequers*;
she's furious at having her *Brexit* proposals spurned,
thrown back in her face by a roomful of compromise-wreckers.
Pipsqueak watches the pound begin sliding towards the deck as
Moggs, *Johnsons* and *Foxes* rejoice that she's brought to heel
and the markets anticipate *Brexit* without a deal.

Top *Edinburgh* lawyers are asking the *Luxemburg Court*
to cut through the fog in which *Article 50* is cloaked;
no provision's laid down and therefore a ruling is sought
on whether, once triggered, the action can be revoked.
Pipsqueak hopes an affirmative answer may come, be invoked,
and as *Brexit Day* looms, with the law at last clearly defined,
the *UK* will pull back, given licence to change her mind.

En route still for *Liverpool*, *Pipsqueak*'s nostrils detect
a sulphurous, turbulent, poisonous stream of hot air;
climatologists say it's the cumulative, noxious effect
of a *National Front* that can form and reform anywhere.
From high above *Birmingham*, *Pipsqueak* looks downward to where
he discerns *UKIP Bulldogs*, loud in their patriot robes,
amid mountains of *Bullshit* piled sky-high by xenophobes.

He'll be back in a week, when the *Tories* meet there to promote
whatever they think will assure them of long-term survival
(though what better to give them a vigorous shake of the throat
than an overdue, welcome, and long-sustained *Labour* revival?)
A breath of fresh *Liverpool* air heralds *Pipsqueak*'s arrival
in the city that knows (how long has this truth been known?)
Walk with hope in your heart and you'll never walk alone.

In *Liverpool* then, *Pipsqueak*'s political hopes lie with *Jezza,*
who offers a programme that's radical, fair and humane,
though it's *Starmer* who's cheered to the rafters when he says a
last minute *People's Vote* might have the option *Remain.*
But at this stage, it's all doubtful – up steps *Unite* to maintain
that a *People's Vote* called, in spite of this to-ing and fro-ing,
will be a straightforward *Yes* or *No* on the terms of our going.

At the moment, it's clear, there's only a hint of a slowdown
in *pro-Brexit* rhetoric, do what *Remainers* are able;
if there's no general election given a *November* showdown,
Labour will back *all the options that lie on the table.*
But uncertainty's toxic and *Pipsqueak*'s cage is unstable;
can *Labour* come up with a policy turnaround
before it's too late and *Pipsqueak*'s cage hits the ground?

Might have is cautious while *will be*'s an emphatic affirmative –
in the *Last Chance Saloon* it's not certain which one will prevail;
between staying and going there is no alternative,
but it's prudent to hold your cards close to your chest in a gale.
No-one can be sure which course will succeed and which fail
though a future with *Europe* gives *Britain* better prospects by far,
so *Pipsqueak*'s glad *Labour's* kept the door marked *Remaining* ajar.

On to *Birmingham* then, where a mountain of *UKIP* hooey
and hard *Brexit* condoms are sanitised out of the way,
though as *Brecht* warned us all at the end of *Arturo Ui*,
the virus is dormant, set to break out another day;
Pipsqueak's treated meanwhile to a remorselessly upbeat display
of small-scale domestic proposals and pleas for unity
against a blue *Tory* backdrop bearing the word *OPPORTUNITY*.

Foreign buyers of *UK* homes will pay a stamp duty surcharge,
and on 60 ft buildings combustible cladding be banned;
the homeless will share major retailers' waste bread and marge
and in another four years, a *Great British Festival's* planned.
Home-grown innovation and culture will rock the land,
while as from today legislation will get to grips
with restaurant proprietors skimming their waiters' tips.

Behind these small hypes there's genuine apprehension –
the *Bullingdon Beast* is about to make his appearance;
the conference hall is shot through with a palpable tension
though what he's been given is only fringe meeting clearance.
It's clear that the prospect of *Boris's* interference
holds conference motionless, paralysed in its sights,
a proverbial rabbit transfixed by oncoming lights.

That oncoming vehicle's driven by selfish *Ambition*
with *Mischief* beside him sprawled in the passenger seat,
behind them ride *Arrogance, Guile* and mute *Inhibition,*
her wrists clamped in handcuffs and gaffer tape wrapped round her feet.
There's a scuffle of minders, then delegates rising to greet
the Member for *Uxbridge/South Ruislip* and (not an *if*, but a *when*)
the prospective hard *Brexit* incumbent of *Number Ten*.

He shows off his scholarship, namedropping *Ibn Khaldoun*,
and *British Caractacus*, chained in the *Rue de la Loi*;
pulls in *praemunire* as something with which to impugn
his pro-*Chequers* rivals, his purpose to scare or annoy.
But for cases like these to count as the *Real McCoy*
an orator ought to make certain he grounds his tropes;
praemunire applied not to all foreign powers but to *Popes*.

In any case back in the sixties that law was repealed;
The Criminal Justice Act (1967) superseded it.
And wherever in *Rome* does the *Rue de la Loi* lie concealed?
Caractacus, even in chains, would surely have heeded it.
He might have drunk hemlock, but luckily never needed it,
schooling *Claudius* so well on all the chance outcomes of strife
he was welcomed to *Rome*, and lived there for the rest of his life.

So the scholarship's dodgy, slanted and primed to impress,
but there's namecalling too, and sentiment, anecdote,
a colloquial, mudslinging mixture it's not hard to guess
is a rhetoric trimmed for a *Prime Ministerial* vote.
(*Pipsqueak* urges less confident demagogue rogues to take note
how alliteration, spread lightly, guides *Britain* towards the exit
with *It's time to chuck Chequers* and *Let's not bottle Brexit.*)

But next day the *Prime Minister* retakes control of the scene
(she's prepared to concede *Boris always puts on a good show*;)
she busts a few moves to the backing of *Dancing Queen*
and once more the pro-*Chequers*, pro-*Tory* hype starts to flow.
With *Brexit* in place, austerity gets the *Heave-ho* –
a policy U-turn that's hailed as a welcome surprise
though they're tears of frustration that well up in *Spreadsheet Phil's* eyes.

Pipsqueak's returned to his cage, relieved to be back on home ground
but he's come to the verge of what's billed as a critical summit.
The radar's gone quiet; all *Pipsqueak* can hear is the sound
of mood music so muted he scarcely dare more than hum it.
Despair fills his heart, but *Pipsqueak* must overcome it;
can *Starmer* and *Cable* between them somehow find a way
to keep *Remain* on the table and so perhaps save the day?

The centre's so loud, and so urgent the pressure to charge in,
push the others aside, and make your own speech to the floor,
that it's easy to overlook what's going on at the margin,
the ten sinister figures grouped just outside your back door.
Their numbers are small but their grip on proceedings is sure;
while the *Tories* may govern, the *DUP* pull the strings
so to *Arlene*, their leader, *Pipsqueak* now turns and sings.

A song

Nunc omnes in commune:

Arlene, squeeze tight, *Arlene*!
Arlene, squeeze tight!
Squeeze tight, *Arlene*, all night, *Arlene*!
They need your votes tonight.

Stringe, Erle-ena!
perstringe strenue!
Severiter, severiter,
suffragia exiguunt!

Melopsit. Strid. solus:

Last summer the *Tories* were struggling
buried up to their necks in the sand;
last summer you came to their rescue,
you sold them a firm helping hand.
(*Nunc omnes etc*, *Arlene*, squeeze tight etc.)

Latine si placet

Alarm bells went off in the kitchen,
blind panic was going the rounds;
the package you sold for their rescue,
it cost them a billion pounds.
(*Nunc omnes etc*, *Arlene*, squeeze tight etc.)

Latine si placet

The *Tories*' hearts beat with pleasure;
the end of their world had come nigh;
but good old *DUP* postponed it
with confidence and supply.
(*Nunc omnes etc*, *Arlene*, squeeze tight etc.)

Latine si placet

For fifteen months *Tories* could manage
to stay up on top of the fight,
and now that *Stormont*'s suspended
a billion quid is alright.
(*Nunc omnes etc*, *Arlene*, squeeze tight etc.)

Latine si placet

Now to preserve the *Good Friday Agreement*
and with it maintain law and order;
both parts of the island of *Ireland*
must keep their invisible border.
(*Nunc omnes etc, Arlene*, squeeze tight etc.) *Latine si placet*

But your solid red line over *Brexit*
brings all *Tory* discussion to heel;
with no *Irish Sea* border backstop
how hamstrung *Conservatives* feel.!
(*Nunc omnes etc, Arlene*, squeeze tight etc.) *Latine si placet*

A rock and a hard place squeeze *Tories*
who shudder and shrink from the pinch;
but hardest of all squeezes *Arlene*,
and *Arlene* won't let up an inch.
(*Nunc omnes etc, Arlene*, squeeze tight etc.) *Latine si placet*

It's not long ago, *Cousin Arlene*,
you sold *Tory* chances a boost
but you'll see pretty soon, *Cousin Arlene*,
those chickens will come home to roost.
(*Nunc omnes etc, Arlene*, squeeze tight etc.) *Latine si placet*

If the *Tories* don't like it or lump it,
they'll huff and they'll puff and they'll frown;
then the *DUP*'s and the *Tories*
will together come tumbling down.
(*Nunc omnes etc, Arlene*, squeeze tight etc.) *Latine si placet*

So – *Arlene*, squeeze tight, *Arlene*!
Arlene, squeeze tight!
Squeeze tight, *Arlene*, all night, *Arlene*!
They need your votes tonight.

27 September–14 October 2018

Part XVI: A bonfire of Brexit vanities

All week eager children have been rattling *Pipsqueak*'s cage
wanting money for fireworks, a *Halloween* trick-or-treat,
and *Pipsqueak* has shown himself keen for his part to engage
with the up-to-the-minute *Whatever's-in-play* of the street;
he doesn't have money but hands over something to eat,
a sliver of cuttle, a choice cube of iodine brick,
a beak'sworth of millet, a finely shaved celery stick.

The children run off, shouting out blessings or curses;
the street fills with coarse language, jibes, merriment, jubilation.
Pipsqueak might have wrapped some of those seasonal gifts in his verses,
these squibs, rockets and screamers touch-papered with indignation;
they'd have gone down a storm in the upcoming conflagration
but they're destined for *Facebook* subscribers and the jumping jack
firecracker catalogue of *Andy Croft*'s luminous *Smokestack*.

Is it too much to hope any parents who come within range
of the crackle and spark from the firepowder packed in these lines
might stand up to challenge the *UK*'s prospectus for change?
Pipsqueak spends every morning perusing the papers for signs
but the political landscape's untroubled by grand designs
for a more liberal Europe, the overthrow of the few,
a re-enfranchised *UK*, an enlightened, reformed *EU*.

Instead, we move further and further towards estrangement,
the actions and language of brutalised disregard;
the *DNA* of our decency's subject to rearrangement,
a model of *Grenfell*'s burnt in a *South London* back yard
and *Mrs May*'s warned not simply to be on her guard
ahead of a backbencher's meeting, nor prepare for abuse,
but as she *enters the killing zone*, to make sure she *brings her own noose.*

The *Demagogue Trump* in a string of impassioned harangues
calls the migrant Hondurans a sinister *Democrat Plot*
to let *unknown Middle Easterners, Bad People*, and *Criminal Gangs*
into *Sovereign America*, whether entitled or not.
But *Pipsqueak* knows perfectly well that the *Truth* isn't what
leads *Demagogue Trump* to propagate fake projections
but fear of defeat in the imminent midterm elections.

And in *Istanbul, Pipsqueak*'s seen unfold something that may be a
reason for rewriting *UK*/international relations
but no doubt we'll carry on selling weapons to *Saudi Arabia*
though a *Consulate* murder's been airbrushed by declarations
of unauthorised hitmen engaged in rogue operations,
and we'll make outrage sufficient at famine on *Yemeni* soil
since starvation costs less than the price of a barrel of oil.

Brexit discussions meanwhile go on in the so-called *tunnel*,
a dark, secret place locked in blackout, the blinds pulled down.
Is there light at its end? Or is it a place where the fun'll
kick off when we leave, a back room in *The Rose and Crown*
where the drink's on the house as we run, or are run, out of town?
Rockets burst in the air, stars flare, and the firmament's split;
Pipsqueak flies from his cage to where *Vanity*'s bonfire is lit.

It's a mountain of bigotry, built on political bunkum,
manifestoes – red, yellow, green, polychrome, purple, and blue;
they've all served their turn and now's come the moment to junk'em
however well truth's mixed with lies and whatever their hue.
The fire catches hold, the judgement flames crackle and spew;
the smoke of roast chestnuts is blended with pumpkin and squash
in a *Totentanz* carnival straight out of *Hieronymus Bosch*.

Birds gather in flocks, but singular as our names
the great *British* people, whether working or making hay,
make the most of the moment and just as soon as the flames
start to lick at the woodwork, our watchword is *Seize the day*.
Since a *February* heatwave may herald a snowfall in *May*
we put on warm coats, balaclavas, and wrap up tight
going onto the street for the fireworks on *Bonfire Night*.

So the world and his wife are watching the bonfire blaze;
Joe Soap and the *Ansty* girls, *John Sidney* and *Shirley Smout,*
June Herring and *Sarah Smiles*, *Tip Dodsley*, *Veronica Craze,*
Sean Finnan and *Aoife*, *Dai Morgan*, and *Corcoran Sprout.*
Errol Freeman is there with the *Proctors*; over there's *Colin Clout,*
Fran Jenkins, *Jane Snodgrass*, *Ajax Moto* and *Rory McReady,*
'Buster' Beale, *E.S.Tover*, the *Conroys* and little *Eddie.*

The night sky is streaked with shells, rockets and coloured streamers;
our political leaders keep watch by the edge of the fire.
The proud, the resolved, the self-serving, the hapless, the schemers,
they have no concrete plans to extinguish the funeral pyre.
And it isn't *Guy Fawkes* perched on top, as the flames mount higher,
but, pale, undernourished and weak, though still recognisably human,
staked, tied, her lips parted in anguish, the effigy of a woman.

Her trident has gone, and the shield at the side of her throne,
her imperial robes are a threadbare and spark-pocked rag;
her temples are lined, her fingers worn down to the bone,
and of her once long flowing tresses there remains little to brag.
But *Britannia*'s still wearing the shreds of the *Union Flag*
and as hatreds burn on, *Pipsqueak* hears her imploring call
through the xenophobe brimstone, *Welcome one, welcome all!*

In the light of the bonfire the *Prime Minister* shuffles her feet,
busting a few practice moves for the dawn of *Agreement Day*;
a choleric *Jezza* asks who's really enjoying the heat,
while *Sir Vince* wrings his hands and turns facing the other way.
First Minister Sturgeon's looking forward to *Hogmanay*,
but *Arlene*'s pure granite, imperturbable as *The Sphinx*;
she's *cut off her eyelids* and won't be the first one who blinks.

The fire flickers on; its rate of combustion is slow;
forty years have gone by since the *Tories* first lit the fuse;
that *Thatcherite* flint struck a spark that soon grew to a glow
and what's happened since then is already yesterday's news.
The fugitive state is convinced it has nothing to lose
but fragmented and quarrelling already bears the cost
of an error-strewn policy, already mourns what it's lost.

Now tomorrow is here and the furious *Demagogue* blaze
of the midterm elections is dampened but not put out;
Dai Morgan's in bed fast asleep with *Veronica Craze*
and *June Herring* is likewise alongside *Corcoran Sprout.*
Jane Snodgrass has breakfast with *Moto* and *Colin Clout*
but *Pipsqueak's* alert; resourceful, bold, undismayed,
he knows the time's come to call in the fire brigade.

A song

The Brexit bonfire's all aflame,
fire creeps towards Britannia's toes;
it's no time to apportion blame,
we need the guys who man the hose!
Are there still heroes worth the name
who'll come to Great Britannia's aid?
We need the guys who'll dowse the flame!
Run quick and call the fire brigade!

pedem in
Britanniam
pervenit ignis
fortissimos viros ad
incendium requiruntur
currite, currite!
Festinate ut patriam
ab incendio eripitis!

The night sky flares with Brexit sparks
the country's full of flame and smoke;
our streets resound to bulldog barks;
we chafe and clamour, gag and choke.
About us all an ill wind blows
and hopes for Great Britannia fade.
We need the guys who'll man the hose!
Run quick and call the fire brigade!

ventus malus
Britanniam
circumspirat

tubuli pleni aquae
incendium
deflammabunt

Pour water on the bonfire stokers!
Fetch hoses! Saturate their logs!
Drench all those eager Brexit brokers,
the Graylings, Foxes, Goves, Rees-Moggs!
The self-styled patriots propose
no limits to our global trade;
but we need guys who'll man the hose!
Run quick and call the fire brigade!

furciferos in aqua
frigida perfundete!

But wait! Our credit's turned to ash
the shires have all gone stony broke,
the country's used up all its cash,
austerity's gone up in smoke.
The fire burns on and no-one knows
who will clear up the mess it's made
if we can't find who'll man the hose,
if we can't call the fire brigade.

pecunia deest;
quomodo igitur
senatores stipendia
aliorum reddere possunt?

5–18 November2018

Part XVII: Draft Withdrawal Agreement disputes

It's the end of *November.* Gales buffet *Pipsqueak*'s cage
and he's tossed from his perch in a jaw-jarring somersault;
he's fitter and nimbler than many birds half his age
so the loss of *Zen Calm* can't be entirely his fault.
But since *Brexit*'s got close he's begun a climacteric moult
of forbearance and plumage as patience begins to fail
and outrage increases with each feather that drops from his tail.

In vain *Pipsqueak* nibbles his nutritious iodine block;
feathers loosen and droop, curled remiges sink to the ground;
the *Withdrawal Agreement* has put him in nervous shock,
an unhappy condition, dark, comfortless and profound.
Past curing by drugs, past treatment by ultrasound,
his only recourse as one bad week leads to a worse
is to remount his perch, sit tall and purge outrage in verse.

There's a lot to be said for versing, whether it's rhyme
or whether plain syllable-counting's what floats your boat;
you can flatter, narrate, sue, riddle, woo, pull for prime,
but complaining and carping are what really get *Pipsqueak*'s vote.
His verses can scarcely stop sounding a *Quarrelsome Note*
given *Buccaneer Tories*, grown headstrong on *Brexit Spliff,*
are dragging the *UK* right to the edge of the cliff.

It's a fortnight since the *Prime Minister* brought *The Draft
Withdrawal Agreement* back home for cabinet scrutiny;
they played ball for a day, but afterwards started to shaft
the terms she'd agreed on, and two rose to mutiny.
McVey pitched in hard, while *Raab* put the boot in; he
himself, *in good conscience,* considered the document sinister,
a cyanide bombshell when dropped by the *Brexit Minister.*

They resigned, were replaced by *Steve Barclay* and *Amber Rudd*;
the *PM* took the draft back to *Brussels* for formal signing.
There were many for *Brexit* who thought the *Agreement* a dud,
a dark thundercloud with no trace of a silver lining.
There was talk of betrayal, talk of the *PM* resigning;
the *Pizza Club* chafed in their takeaway impotence
and *Rees-Mogg* view-hallooed a vote of no confidence.

It wasn't forthcoming. Just how many signatures short
of the 48 needed, only *The Sun* could guess;
the *PM* stood firm, urging *Parliament* to support
a compromise deal, but our best deal nevertheless.
Pipsqueak from his perch watched hostility coalesce;
in the street, in the *Commons*, few spoke up to applaud her,
few bought her backstop fudge for the *Irish* border.

That evergreen issue, otherwise red, white and blue,
saw anger intensify, rhetoric escalate;
should the *Six Counties* post-*Brexit* remain within the *EU*
or with once-great *Great Britain* become part of a *Vassal State*?
These were options no *Bowler Hat* could contemplate,
and few others either; the patriot chips were down,
and the *Prime Minister*'s executive aircraft was first out of town.

She set off at once on a *UK*-wide charm offensive,
in *Cardiff* and *Belfast* praising the thing to the skies;
in *Scotland* she gave little sign of becoming defensive
looking hostile detractors and nitpickers straight in the eyes.
But her relentless, repetitive marketing could not disguise
mistrust of the document, widespread dissent, disaffection,
a groundswell of discontent foreshadowing its rejection.

She went on to address the *G20 Summit* in *Argentina*
(a platform where planning for mutual benefit thrives);
Britain's grass after *Brexit*, she said, would be notably greener
yet nobody swept to her side to engage in high fives.
Pipsqueak will be astonished (and gutted) if she survives
Showdown Tuesday's result a week hence in the *Lions' Den*
given the *No to no deal* amendment proposed by *Hilary Benn.*

This elegant stratagem, backed by both *Lib Dems* and *SNP*,
drops *No deal* and *May's deal* alike like a ton of bricks;
it leaves open a way for the *Commons* themselves to agree
on a better way forward than either side's parcel of tricks.
It would be splendid to see *Project Fear* at last clattered for six,
and *Project Compromise* also despatched to the boundary exit;
Pipsqueak hopes it might signal the death-knell of *Project Brexit*.

The whole *Brexit* saga has gone on for quite long enough;
the future is bleak, the political climate surreal.
Does anyone think *President Tusk* is indulging in bluff
when he says if *May* loses it's *No Brexit* or else it's *No deal*?
All agree that the second of these carries little appeal;
the *Treasury* sees the economy running aground,
Threadneedle Street forecasts recession, a spiralling pound.

Pipsqueak's moulting goes on but he'd far better live in hope
than fill buckets of water after the milk's been spilt;
a cage packed knee-deep in his feathers gives plenty of scope
for a warm padded waistcoat, a fifteen tog winter quilt.
Best demolish the sandcastle mansion that *Mrs May*'s built;
it's damp and unheated, the roof leaks, it's not worth the rent;
join *Pipsqueak* instead in this outburst of merriment.

A Song

The *Brexit Bells* go ting-a-ling-a-ling,
for you but not for me;
Theresa, where's thy sting-a-ling-a-ling?
O *May,* thy victory?

Johnson has had his fling-a-ling-a-ling
with you but not with me;
O *Boris* you won't bring-a-ling-a-ling,
your side to victory.

victoria a tali homine
nunquam capietur!

The *Brexit Bells* go ding-a-ling-a-ling,
for you but not for me;
Theresa, where's thy sting-a-ling-a-ling?
O *May,* thy victory?

Rees-Mogg has done his thing-a-ling-a-ling
for you but not for me;
but *Jacob* can't quite swing-a-ling-a ling,
that sought-for victory.

octo et quadraginta
suffragia necesse erant;
satis eorum non accessit J.R-M.

Chorus

Here comes *Grayling* Gray-ling-a-ling-a-ling
arriving late again;
his *Brexit* plan's failing-a-ling-a-ling
he's missed the *Brussels* train.

connexionem suam
non attetegit Cenericulus.

Chorus

Come gather in a ring-a-ling-a-ling
and huddle round the stove;
the herald angels sing-a-ling-a-ling
to comfort *Michael Gove.*

angeli caduceatores circum
craticulam Govii lachrymas
fictas deflent.

Chorus

The last round bell goes ting-a-ling-a-ling,
the champ goes down for three;
though Brexit's still her thing-a-ling-a-ling,
she's far from victory.

oppugnat Theresa,
quanquam
causa sua
perdita videtur...

28 November–3 December 2018

Part XVIII: The Meaningful Vote is deferred

Pipsqueak's mirror's attached by a clip to the bars of his cage;
he can use it for grooming wherever he stands on his perch;
a lunge, stretch or shimmy and *Pipsqueak* is able to gauge
the best way to remove a disfiguring smudge, stain or smirch.
Its convex periphery makes the meticulous search
of *Pipsqueak*'s environs a labour of consummate ease;
there's no hiding place in his plumage for lice, ticks or fleas.

Six times a day, morning, afternoon, evening, he draws
himself up to the mirror, ensuring his shoulders are level;
he bows, fluffs his coat, shakes a leg, fettles his claws
this way and that before the omnivorous bevel.
With cut, peck and scrape he sends parasites to the devil,
ventilates his remiges, voids the heat from his frame,
and seven days a week, six times a day, does the same.

All this and more *Pipsqueak*'s readers might well expect,
since they too use mirrors to shave in and part their hair;
it's the work of a mirror to take hold of, to frame and reflect
the uncoloured, uncompromised look of one's personal stare.
But this mirror of *Pipsqueak*'s has no equal anywhere;
it's an heirloom passed down from Master *John Skelton* of *Diss*;
a true witness of folly, a *speculum temporis*.

It reveals the misdeeds of each wicked and mischievous age;
it gave *Skelton*'s parrot the power and permisson to prate,
stoked a fire in his spleen and quickened his heart to engage,
to censure and satirise, savage and castigate.
The *Poet* and *Parrot* were *Furies Confederate*
who seeing our follies so plainly exposed in their mirror
summoned invective, wit, learning to purge and to cauterise error.

Skelton's parrot passed on, and the poet himself likewise
went in due course to his *Maker*, as all poets must.
But *Satire*'s bright beacon once set alight never dies,
though author and subject alike be compounded with dust;
Fame joins with *Destiny* sparing the mirror from rust
and centuries later, *Pipsqueak* picks up once again
the crazed silver surface, the coarse-gritted edge of the tain.

He can call it to life with invective or erudition,
from his polyglot archive deploying a curse or a prayer;
the *speculum*'s programmed with up-to-date *Squeak Recognition*
giving access to *Outrage* in all weathers everywhere.
What the mirror reveals would make many budgies despair
but *Pipsqueak*'s resourceful, resilient, hard as nails,
and *Mischief* must go to the wall where his satire prevails.

There are barely three days to go now before *Showdown Tuesday*
which the mirror reveals is billed also as *May's Last Stand*;
the prologue this week was a decidedly epic bad news day
for a leadership wanting to market the *Brexit* scheme planned.
The start of their sales pitch saw the *Government* panned
for *Contempt* of the *Commons,* having not disclosed several
key items of *Brexit* advice set down by the *Attorney General.*

This true-to-life *Rumpole* took the part of the indefensible,
maintaining the right to keep legal cards close to his chest;
the *Commons* considered his argument reprehensible
despite high-flown calls on the *National Interest*;
his performance that day was one of pantomime's best,
a stick-wielding stage-villain making the peasants squeal
with *Stop baying and shouting* (pause); (louder) *Grow up, and get real.*

The full text of his counsel the following day revealed
he thought the backstop if invoked might prove permanent
and that market arrangements would unbalance the playing field
between mainland *UK*, *Belfast*, and the *Continent*.
The prospect of border checks and *UK* dismemberment
saw the red mist come down, and cross-party opinion glad
to unite in the view that *Mrs May*'s *Brexit* was bad.

The *Commons* have ruled that, should they tomorrow defeat
Mrs May's plan for *Brexit,* they'll be the ones to decide
how best to engage with the hopes of the man in the street,
and devise some third way to bring dissident factions onside.
Moreover, the *EU* now rules that the *UK* is justified
in withdrawing from *Brexit* alone in peremptory smoke;
what a sovereign state calls on, a sovereign state may revoke.

As a result of all this the climate of *Brexit* has changed;
there's a glimmer of light, *UK* prospects are not quite so scanty;
our contract for substandard goods can be rearranged
with an option in place to revert to the *status quo ante.*
But the moment's not come to rejoice and uncork the *Chianti*;
Pipsqueak turns to his mirror; aghast, though the imagery's blurred,
he picks out the newsflash – *Tomorrow's vote is deferred.*

* * * *

The country's in turmoil. The *Prime Minister*'s pulled the plug
on a vote she admitted she'd lose *by a significant margin*;
after three days of controversy, whipcracking, rhetorical humbug,
the battle she sought, it was clear, would be fatal to charge in.
Her *Number 10* tea leaves spelled out *menetekel upharshin*;
so she's drawn back from the precipice rather than take a hit,
though the *Bolsover Beast* observed, rather more bluntly, *She's frit.*

It's been clear for three months that *Mrs May*'s job's on the line
now the *Chequers* agenda's got stuck in the back of her throat;
that *Conservative Bluster* is what has come to define
her leadership style, though that's small cause for *Labour* to gloat;
how long will it take for a *Labour* no-confidence vote
to be put and be carried, this smug, reprehensible shower
of faux-democrat *Tories* be swept chafing headlong from power?

* * * *

The improbable's happened. What *Pipsqueak* cried out for last night
is today's headline news, a storm blown from a *Tory* quarter;
May's moment of truth has arrived, much to *Pipsqueak*'s delight,
and *Tory MPs* must today depose or support her.
Pipsqueak's verses tonight will be made with fresh bricks and mortar;
for the moment, however, one key question vexes his brain:-
Has *Johnson* endured that pre-*Christmas* haircut in vain?

* * * *

It's a win, not a triumph. She's 83 votes *over the line*
with 117 *Tory MPs* having signalled their disaffection;
for the moment she's safe, but so far she's given no sign
of *rapprochement* or thaw, much less a change of direction.
She says she'll step down before the next *General Election*
though when that might be is well beyond anyone's guessing;
no-one's blinking in *Brussels*, and *Starmer* is already pressing.

All *Pipsqueak* can do is resume his complaining and wait
for the vote to return to the floor of the *House* as it must;
will the *New Year* see the *Prime Minister* given checkmate
and a rebranded, cosmeticised *Brexit* plan crumble to dust?
With the *Commons* in gridlock, who is there for *Pipsqueak* to trust?
While *Downing Street* gestures, and *Westminster*'s quarrels rage
there's cold comfort for *Pipsqueak*, as *Brexit* winds buffet his cage.

Times are hard and depressing, the air's loud with *Politicos* scrapping,
a *Bone* of contention pits *Hammond* against *Rees-Mogg*
but from out in the street *Pipsqueak* catches the rhythm of rapping.
He looks in his mirror, and just visible through the fog
there's a gangsta-rap figure – is it *Busta Rhymes, 50 Cent*, or *Snoop Dogg?*
and he's flossing his talk. To *Pipsqueak* it's an inspiration,
so he breaks out a few verbs of his own to spice up a conversation.

A song

Who am I who am I what's my name?
The bird with the word I'm him I'm the same,
Quis avis quis avis? kiss kiss don't mess ain't you heard?
I'm *Pipsqueak Pipsqueak* the bird you heard
A strong bird a strong bird not weak
When I squeak you hear me speak I don't shriek
Da Da / Da Da Da / Hey Hey / Hey Hey /Da Da

Who am I who am I what's my name?
The bird with the word the same bird in the hall of fame
In speculo temporis that's me where the mirror is
Not playin this *Brexit* game
This *Brexit* game it's shame it's a shame shame shame
Pipsqueak's a strong bird don't say a wrong word
Not playing this *Brexit* game you heard yes you heard
Da Da / Da Da Da / Hey Hey / Hey Hey /Da Da

Who am I who am I what's my name?
Cottonpickin *Tories* you take the blame
Take the blame blame for this *Brexit* game
Nobody choosin everyone losin losin losin
Nobody choosin the *Brexit* game
Avem audivistis tristis tristis you heard yes you heard the bird
You heard the word on the street
You heard the word defeat
Defeat's the word on the street
Play this *Brexit* game you end up on the street
Play this *Brexit* game you end up with no name no name
Da Da / Da Da Da / Hey Hey / Hey Hey /Da Da

Who am I who am I what's my name?
Peep out this *Brexit* game
Nebulous nebulous nebulous
Who gives you that name?
Sack that *Brexit* dame send back that dame
Mulierem dimittete have no pity
Don't play that game that's no shame
Brexit game is a cryin shame that's no lyin
No cryin no cryin keep tryin
Cottonpickin *Tories* to blame keep lyin
You losin losin nobody choosin
You heard the word
You end up with no name
You don't speak you take the blame
You speak you speak no *Brexit* game
No *Brexit* game no no no no *Brexit* game

Da Da / Da Da Da / Hey Hey / Hey Hey /Da Da
Da Da / Da Da Da / Hey Hey / Hey Hey /Da Da
Da Da / Da Da Da / Hey Hey / Da Da /Hey Hey

6–16 December 2018

Part XIX: Lipreading Corbyn

It's the last game before *Christmas* in *Brexitville*'s *Westminster Park*;
the *Reds* are one down and match tempo has started to drag;
the *Blues* keep the ball to themselves in the gathering dark
and the clock's running down to full time by the corner flag.
It's not yet all over, the game isn't yet in the bag,
but the *Reds* are dejected and *Captain Jezza's* been booked;
one more yellow card and their *Christmas Goose* will be cooked.

The game's been bad-tempered, with players showing little respect
for the rules, for opponents, team colleagues, coach, linesman or ref;
there's been elbowing, diving, bad-mouthing deployed to project
every word in *The Brexiteer's Phrasebook* beginning with *F.*
To appeals from the stands the belligerent players are deaf;
disenchanted *Reds* fans won't be singing under the mistle-
toe on the terraces once the ref blows the final whistle.

Instead, in the *Westminster Arms* or *St Stephen's Tavern*
they'll sit with a shandy, a *Guinness*, a large rum and coke,
and deep in the gloom of their underground *Stygian* cavern
bemoan *Jezza*'s failings – *No doubt he's a nice enough bloke*
and his rhetoric's fine, but his on-pitch performance? A joke.
He's too fond of a back pass, holds onto the ball too much,
and when a scoring chance beckons, he wellies the ball into touch.

He's the same in the *Commons*, setting up a no-confidence motion
in the *Prime Minister* but not (yet) in the *Government* as a whole;
the *Blues* rightly considered this merely a drop in the ocean,
a pre-*Christmas* snowflake dropped into a finger-bowl;
they allowed the *Reds' Captain* to notch up a neat own goal
by declining *for lack of time* to make time to address
his motion at all this side of the *Christmas* recess.

Worse was to follow. Last week at *Prime Minister's Questions*
the *Blue Captain* dropped into seasonal pantomime mode;
the *Blue Team* picked up on her *O yes he did* suggestions
but *Jez* mouthed the words *Stupid woman,* and the words showed;
he claimed afterwards he'd said *people* but the episode
was ill-humoured, embarrassing, demeaning, distracting, corrosive,
and the video replay confirmed a marked shortage of plosive.

Pipsqueak back in the day learned *Phonetics* while studying *Mimicry,*
the subtle articulation of alveolar-palatal-dental
which gained him the skill to puncture political gimmickry
and expose banal thought masquerading as transcendental;
Jezza used the word *woman*, a term in this context detrimental
to all norms of *Civility*, all forms of *Mutual Respect,*
rude, sexist, discourteous and *Politically Incorrect.*

It created a storm of protest and indignation,
accusations, denials, procedural quibbles, fudges;
the chamber grew loud with cross-party recrimination,
the verdicts of expert, impartial, deaf, lip-reading judges.
What humans dispute is perfectly clear to budgies,
and *pace* the *Speaker*, *Pipsqueak*'s convinced it's absurd
to believe an *MP* on the sole grounds that he's given his word.

The storm sidelined issues in need of immediate action –
child poverty, homelessness, mismanaged benefits, cuts
to hospital services, schools, the police, the distraction
of government so lacking political heart or the guts
to be wise, caring and generous that it shuts
the door on compassion and, full of its own conceit,
lets children go hungry, adults freeze to death on the street.

It spends billions of pounds funding so-called contingency plans
as the *UK*'s bleak day of reckoning comes into view;
there'll be soldiers to muffle the clatter of pots and pans
striking pavements and kerbs should we finally bid the *EU*
a noisy, ungrieving and ill-judged no-deal adieu;
small businesses are advised to secure *EORI* registration,
make software arrangements, upgrade their administration.

The reality is that the contingency plans are designed
not just to allay, but as much to exacerbate fear,
their immediate purpose to challenge and focus the mind
of the *Commons* ahead of the *Meaningful Vote* held next year.
With chaos in prospect and small hope of longer term cheer
will *Parliament* vote for an unmapped or a roughly sketched land?
the bird in the bush, or the *Prime Minister's* bird in the hand?

Pipsqueak hopes that the *Commons* kick out the existing proposal
and offer instead a fresh *Leave /Remain* plebiscite;
that *Labour* deploy all the arguments at their disposal
in support of *Remain*, and put up a vigorous fight;
that after years of division, the *UK* will once more unite
with a future in *Europe*, a step-changing re-connect
based on reason, compassion, tolerance, renewed respect.

Christmas morning is here, and the precincts of *Pipsqueak*'s cage,
loud with resonant carols, are seasonal, festive and jolly;
were *Pipsqueak* a parrot, like that bird of an earlier age,
you'd receive parcels of nutmeg labelled *From Pretty Polly.*
But *Pipsqueak*'s a budgie, stern critic of humbug and folly,
so, mindful as ever that self-indulgence is wrong,
instead of a nutmeg he sings you this *Christmas* song:

A song

On the first day of Christmas my true love sent to me
a bright shiny pro-Remain MP.

Gratias, pulcherrima!

On the second day of Christmas my true love sent to me
two cautious Corbyns
and a bright shiny pro-Remain MP.

Gratias, pulcherrima!

On the third day of Christmas my true love sent to me
three hapless Hammonds
two cautious Corbyns
and a bright shiny pro-Remain MP.

Gratias, pulcherrima!

On the fourth day of Christmas my true love sent to me
four furtive Foxes
three hapless Hammonds
two cautious Corbyns
and a bright shiny pro-Remain MP.

Gratias, pulcherrima!

On the fifth day of Christmas my true love sent to me
five grafting Goves;
four furtive Foxes
three hapless Hammonds
two cautious Corbyns
and a bright shiny pro-Remain MP.

Gratias, pulcherrima!

On the sixth day of Christmas my true love sent to me
six silken Rees-Moggs
five grafting Goves;
four furtive Foxes
three hapless Hammonds
two cautious Corbyns
and a bright shiny pro-Remain MP.

Gratias, pulcherrima!

On the seventh day of Christmas my true love sent to me
seven Bercows barking
six silken Rees-Moggs
five grafting Goves;
four furtive Foxes
three hapless Hammonds
two cautious Corbyns
and a bright shiny pro-Remain MP.

Gratias, pulcherrima!

On the eighth day of Christmas my true love sent to me
eight failing Graylings
seven Bercows barking
six silken Rees-Moggs
five grafting Goves;
four furtive Foxes
three hapless Hammonds
two cautious Corbyns
and a bright shiny pro-Remain MP.

Gratias, pulcherrima!

On the ninth day of Christmas my true love sent to me
nine Mays a-milking
eight failing Graylings
seven Bercows barking
six silken Rees-Moggs
five grafting Goves;
four furtive Foxes
three hapless Hammonds
two cautious Corbyns
and a bright shiny pro-Remain MP.

Gratias, pulcherrima!

On the tenth day of Christmas my true love sent to me
ten Brexit Bowlers
nine Mays a-milking
eight failing Graylings
seven Bercows barking
six silken Rees-Moggs
five grafting Goves;
four furtive Foxes
three hapless Hammonds
two cautious Corbyns
and a bright shiny pro-Remain MP.

Gratias, pulcherrima!

On the eleventh day of Christmas my true love sent to me
eleven Leadsoms looming
ten Brexit Bowlers
nine Mays a-milking
eight failing Graylings
seven Bercows barking
six silken Rees-Moggs
five grafting Goves;
four furtive Foxes
three hapless Hammonds
two cautious Corbyns
and a bright shiny pro-Remain MP.

Gratias, pulcherrima!

On the twelfth day of Christmas my true love sent to me
twelve Johnsons jesting
eleven Leadsoms looming
ten Brexit Bowlers
nine Mays a-milking
eight failing Graylings
seven Bercows barking
six silken Rees-Moggs
five grafting Goves;
four furtive Foxes
three hapless Hammonds
two cautious Corbyns

and a bright shiny pro-Remain MP.

Gratias tibi pulcherrima maxime, maxime ago!

20–25 December 2018

Part XX: Cross-Channel traffic is a matter of concern

The *New Year* for *Pipsqueak* is often a laid-back affair,
a time for beak-buffing, slow preening, tucking into an iodine block
before mounting his perch and gazing vacantly into thin air
while *Eternity* measures her hours to an unhurried clock.
It's a time for reflection, digestion, a few days of taking stock;
while fireworks explode in a spectacular crackle of touch
Pipsqueak's ensconced in his cage and not doing anything much.

But this year's been special – a new year full of surprises
turns *Astonishment* loose to shake all the birds on the street;
Amazement runs riot (and *Pipsqueak* just can't disguise his)
at a celestial triumph, a grand-scale astronomical feat.
As discoveries go, this is a hard one to beat,
knocking everyone sideways from *Demagogue Trump* to *Yours truly*;
a space probe launched thirteen years back has reached *Ultima Thule.*

Pipsqueak himself is a master of improvised flight,
a precision exponent of corkscrew turn, take-off and landing;
to see *Pipsqueak* soar, swerve, undulate, dive, and alight
as though dancing on air is enlightening, mind-expanding;
but the breathtaking grace of his choreography notwithstanding,
New Horizons breaks records for distance, speed, pitch-and-yaw steering,
computerised flight control, state-of-the-art engineering.

A *Kuiper Belt Object*, barely twenty miles long by six,
a snowman-shaped ice-block some four billion miles from our planet,
it's thought tiny *Thule* might still hold the *Original Mix*
of our post-*Big Bang* world before *Primitive Life* overran it.
At unbelievable speed and with only split seconds to scan it,
the probe as it passed amassed mountains of data to shatter
the unresolved riddle of how *Life* arose out of *Matter*.

For the next sixteen months *New Horizons* will patiently send
pictures, soundings and measurements straight back to *NASA HQ*;
astrophysicists there predict no foreseeable end
in the decades ahead to the data that will accrue
once *Thule*'s downloaded and other worlds come into view;
small wonder, therefore, *Earth* hastens to mark the day
with a new verse from *Pipsqueak*, a new song from *Brian May*.

What's a verse after all but the music sent spiralling back
from the avian heart by a pestering bird with the gift
of a probing imagination steadied and kept on track
by a passion for order of sorts and an inclination to sift
the grain from the chaff just as well on a graveyard shift
as on days bright with invention, a salvo to rock humanity
with a glimpse of some brave new world or a riff on its vanity?

Come today, come tomorrow, and *Pipsqueak* shifts round on his perch,
turns his back on the skies and once more confronts *terra firma*;
the *Government*'s picked up on its cack-handed pre-*Christmas* search
for some *Brexit* solution against which few critics might murmur.
But two things in its strategy make *Pipsqueak* squirm:- a
so-called *Major Incident* with which we must get to grips,
and a contract for freight ferries passed to a firm with no ships.

Certain small groups of migrants are crossing the *Channel* in boats
you'd be foolish to sail across calm recreational water;
shipping lanes are a threat to any small vessel that floats
without coastguard or lifeboat or *Border Force* craft to escort her.
The *UK*'s anti-immigrant wind blows from a hostile quarter,
and cutting his holidays short *Home Secretary Javid's* stance
is that cross-*Channel* bound refugees should remain in *France*.

He stresses the dangers involved in a hazardous crossing,
the perils conspiring to stop migrants from reaching our shore,
the extortionate payments demanded by traffickers tossing
the least scruple overboard for *€3,000* and more;
then *hysteron proteron* he wonders *But can we be sure*
that these people in dinghies, unfortunate migrants in name,
are truly the genuine refugees that they claim?

Shame on you, *Javid!* The dangers are real enough,
and so is the money demanded by trafficking gangs,
but you're disfiguring truth with this disingenuous stuff;
your tongue-in-cheek rhetoric can't hide its poisonous fangs.
You know perfectly well that refugee status hangs
on a request for asylum placed in the government's hands
of the country in which the fugitive finally lands.

We take far less than our share of people in need of a refuge,
pitching minimal gains against sovereign identity lost;
we ramp up the ante by calling a trickle a deluge
and sideline discussion of all opportunity cost.
In the migrations of argument, somewhere a boundary's crossed;
the warm-hearted, generous host is replaced by a sentry
and the sign that once read *Welcome Aboard* now reads *No Entry.*

So much for the xenophobes. *Pipsqueak*'s credulity's stretched
by a pre-*Brexit* plan to forestall any transport emergency
you might at this stage consider unlikely, far-fetched;
we're commissioning firms to provide *as a matter of urgency*
additional ferries to set up and run a resurgent sea-
crossing freight service from *Ramsgate* to *Ostende,*
a component, long term, of our *Post-Brexit Dividend.*

The lion's share of the contract has gone to *Brittany Ferries*
and *DFDS* in more or less equal amounts
and no-one begrudges these firms the pick of the cherries,
given strong trading records, prime assets, transparent accounts.
But it's hard to see how *Commissioner Grayling* surmounts
the modest objection (it's whispered on everyone's lips)
that his third favoured firm, *Seaborne Freight*, is a firm with no ships.

To be sure, it's a drawback, but *Management Speak* can get round it
by making it seem that a not-yet-signed deal's in the bag;
if the truth's inconvenient, let an opportune sea fret surround it,
and bring wishful thinking on board to massage a snag;
dress shortcomings up as achievements of which you can brag,
and delete from your website, as soon as ever you may,
those terms and conditions skanked from *Joe's Takeaway.*

The last week of *March* was their deadline to get services going
but mid-*January*'s here, and yesterday *Seaborne* confessed
that despite all their efforts to set *Project Freightferries* flowing
there'll be nothing until the back end of *April* at best.
The *Mayor* of *Ostend* and the *Council* of *Thanet* have stressed
that contracts with *Seaborne* are still a good way from gilt-edged.
(And the harbour at *Ramsgate* still remains to be dredged.)

The *Commons* are back and the *Brexit* debate's been renewed,
there are four days to go ahead of the *Meaningful Vote*;
cross-party exchanges are ugly, ill-tempered and rude
and *Patriot Bigots* hold knives to *Democracy*'s throat.
The air's full of poison but where is the antidote?
Outside the *Commons*, right wing thugs congregate
not to heckle *MPs* but to mob and intimidate.

Our *Brexit* predicament's let loose the beast from the midden;
its xenophobe rhetoric carries us all to the brink
of a perilous cliff where the psychopomp monster we've ridden
can't conceal its indifference whether we swim or we sink;
Pipsqueak sings of a time when each of us comes to re-think
the ill-will he shows towards neighbour, fellow-human and brother,
and at last learns to love, not despise him, because he is other.

A song

The *Channel* is wide, you cannot cross over,
you have no wings with which to fly;
but here's a boat that's bound for *Dover*;
you'll land in *Dover* by and by.

Navis M. Striduli semper
ad navigandum parata est.

It's purpose-built of *English* oak
with *British* sailcloth fore and aft;
its oars proclaim with every stroke
a sturdy, safe, seaworthy craft.

Quam quercus Brittanicus
nihil fortior.

Her crew the strongest, stoutest hearts
that ever graced this sceptered isle;
her skipper, skilled in all the arts
of seamanship, a xenophile.

Dux nauticus
sodalitiumque eius
alienis benevoli sunt.

So farewell now to *Calais* beaches
and farewell now to *Dunkirk* sands,
our way lies where the wide sea reaches
and *England* waits with open hands.

Vale, Caletum!
Au revoir Dunquerca!
iter longum ad
Britanniam est sed cordes
nostrae recte iam ibi sunt.

Across the sea our vessel skips
and insubstantial *Ramsgate* ghosts
salute from phantom motherships
the migrant guests of migrant hosts.

Animae Tanatae
migrationem salutant
hospites hospitem pariter.

No hostile immigrant controls
make seaside games of hide and seek;
no ruthless *Border Force* patrols
will turn back *Omar, Reem, Sadiq*.

Apodidrascinda
nunquam luditur
vigiliae hospites non avertunt.

On *Pipsqueak*'s boat you're safe in *Dover*,
a passing raincloud dims your eye;
the *Channel* 's wide but you've crossed over,
and you've no further need to fly.

Dubrim pertinemus,
ibique refugium
invenitur.

One day, some day, we'll all be free
to walk in through an open door,
blind prejudice be lost at sea
and welcome sound along our shore.

Cum in mare
praejudicium demersitur,
quis illud eriperebit?

4–12 January 2019

Part XXI: After the Meaningful Vote

A great flock of geese has appeared above *Pipsqueak*'s cage,
a quarrelsome, swarming host of stentorian birds;
the air's loud with their wing-beats, thick with aggressive language,
and *Pipsqueak*'s domain is disfigured with green goose-turds.
This morning he's holding his breath, lost (almost) for words
to encipher the brouhaha goose-blather, the tumult, the stink
of ubiquitous ordure so strong he can scarcely think.

These are delegate geese, cohorts of representative fowl
for *British Bird Species* the length and breadth of the land
– chough, sparrow and gannet, dove, heron, kestrel and owl,
the birds in the bush as well as the bird in the hand;
thrush, magpie and chaffinch, lark, duck, woodpecker, sand-
piper, the bird in the cage, on the branch, on the loose,
every five years have chosen their joint representative goose.

Pipsqueak witnessed a *Goose Pledge* to deliver avian prosperity;
the *Privileged Geese* painted pictures of long-term bliss
on condition he put up with painful short-term austerity
and entrusted his cage to their treacherous cackle and hiss.
He didn't believe them – and something indeed was amiss;
the *Privileged Geese* fell to infighting when the need came
to divert opposition, keep control, and find others to blame.

Some blamed the banks, some the markets, many the *Working Geese*
who decades before had enjoyed a ruling majority;
but the mischief each made had been handed on piece by piece,
and they'd all played their part in engendering nationwide poverty.
The search for a scapegoat became a *PG* priority;
certain *Privileged Geese* found a target for hostile words –
the *UK* had suffered an influx of *Alien Birds*.

It was, they maintained, due to membership of a club
to which the *UK* for the past forty years had belonged;
the *Avian Congress of Europe*, they said, was the nub
of a process of stealth by which all our rights had been wronged;
Head Privileged Goose, rather than stomach prolonged
dissent in his cohort did what he claimed was right
and gave *UK* birds a stay-or-go plebiscite.

There were numerous benefits the *Avian Congress* conferred
on its constituent states – the free movement of avian labour,
no tariffs on sandpaper, cuttlefish, millet, and every bird
able to serve, and *Europe*-wide serving, the needs of his neighbour.
The *Pan-European Community* of *Birds* had long since learned to savour
joint nest-building projects, bird safety, research into avian health,
the accumulation of nest-eggs, the slow growth of avian wealth.

Posh Gander no doubt thought the outcome a foregone conclusion;
aware of the benefits, most birds would opt to remain;
the result when it came threw politics into confusion,
rocked the tops of the trees and set spinning the weathervane.
In the teeth of the gale what could *Pipsqueak* do but complain?
Forty-eight percent voted to stay, fifty-two opted to leave;
from folly and error *Pipsqueak* knew there was no reprieve.

Posh Gander resigned, his place taken by *Mother Goose*,
her position confirmed in a subsequent all-bird election;
(*Pipsqueak* claw-marked a *Worker*, while wondering what was the use
when the roundabout nests always looked in another direction;)
Mother Goose, a remainer, gave the *Verdict to Leave* her protection,
spending month after month casting about and about
amid all the grain in the farmyard to find a way out.

She made upbeat announcements, did endless to-ing and fro-ing
to *Congress* headquarters in *Brussels*, where under the banner
of *Avian Freedom* she'd triggered the date of our going.
The date was determined, but when the time came to plan a
mode of departure, more factions disputed the manner
than there were months left for argument, days for debate in the week;
every goose in the farmyard had a *How-we-should leave* in its beak.

Nothing silenced the cackle and honk of the quarrelsome flock –
some said we should leave come what may on the settled date;
some listened aghast to the furious tick of the clock
that robbed *Mother Goose* of time left to negotiate;
some geese found departure too awful to contemplate
and ransacked the deeds of the farmyard in search of a way
to knock *Go* on the head, thwart the *Will* of the *Birds*, and stay.

The deal *Mother Goose* struck she claimed was the best we would manage;
the flock didn't like it, and said so; she came back for more;
she came at them hard, using argument, scaremongering, *gavage*;
some swallowed, some choked, some gagged, and some cast their craw.
But a two-to-one verdict against was the final score;
it was time for *Head Working Goose* to come down off the fence
and table the motion *This flock has no confidence.*

The *Privileged Geese* survived, largely thanks to the backing
of their loyalist partners, the *Protestant Ulstergoose Group*,
ten grit-grinding birds who, however much they were lacking
in good will and good humour, nonetheless governed the coop.
Their power over *Mother Goose* had them all cock-a-hoop;
with the government challenged, not many cared to gainsay
the *Ulstergoose* proverb, *Where there's a quill there's a way.*

So now is the time latent anger has come to the boil –
more debate, more dissension, the farmyard in disarray;
Pipsqueak's panic-proof cage is pitched about in the moil
of pan-anserine clamour, goose mayhem, unbridled affray.
The tyrannical clock counts the hours down to *Reckoning Day*
when *UK Bird Species* – chough, sparrow, kestrel and owl –
must resume once again the mantle of *Insular Fowl.*

The purlieus of *Pipsqueak*'s cage see the furious hackles
of angry geese raised in an orgy of mutual pecking;
he recoils on his perch from their strident, cacophonous cackles,
and the excrement stench that wafts hour by hour from his decking.
His delegate geese are turned delegate *Experts* in *Wrecking*,
unable, so late, to do more than deny the *Goose Mother*
the deal she still wants, and then quarrel with one another.

But it needn't be so. *Pipsqueak* asks every constituent goose
to set difference aside, take a step towards moderation;
set an example to others by declaring an interim truce
and as they once did, respect the whole population.
Should we stay? Should we go? The issue still vexes the nation;
only it can decide, as the implications of each become plain,
in the interests of all, whether we leave or remain.

Here's a song to conclude; an exchange between two hungry crows
Pipsqueak heard while exploring the gridlocked approaches to *Dover*;
the lyrics were plaintive, leading *Pipsqueak* at once to suppose
the two hungry corvids some distance from living in clover.
Stacked lorries belched fumes; drivers cursed long delays and moreover
layby portaloos leaked, but *Pipsqueak*'s nerves remained strong;
the two corbies chattered, and here's what he made of their song.

A song

As *Pipsqueak* walked out all alone he heard two corbies making moan, the one unto the other say, 'Where shall we two dine today?	*Dum M. Stridulus solus* *ambulavit duo corvos audivit.* *Rogavit unus 'amice,* *ubi nos duo prandebimus?'*
'At the foot of yonder cliff there lies *Britannia* cold and stiff and no-one knows that she lies there but *Rag*, and *Tag*, and *Bobtail* fair.	*Responsit amicus 'Ut Britannia* *sub radice rupis mortua est* *nemine scitur praeter* *sentinam civitatis.*
'*Rag*'s gone from home and fled abroad *Tag*'s locked in *Wormwood Scrubs* for fraud and *Bobtail*'s homeless on the street so we may make our dinner sweet.	*'Sentina vel peregre* *fugitiva vel sine domo* *in vinculis vel* *plateatim vivat.*
'You'll dine upon her slate-grey eye, my feast shall be her milk-white thigh; we'll take locks of her coal-black hair to thatch our nest when it grows bare.	*'Tu oculos suos quasi* *cinereas scandulas edes;* *ego coxendicam lacteam* *edam; anthracinum* *crinis capiemus ut nidulum* *nudum tegemus.*
'All mourn the beauty that has been, none find her on the farther shore; o'er her white bones, when they're picked clean, the wind shall blow for evermore.'	*'Omnes puchritudinem* *perditam suam defleunt;* *nemo cadaverem* *in campis elysiis inveniebit.* *Ventus super ossa candida* *per saecula saeculorum aspirabit.'*
As *Pipsqueak* walked out all alone he heard two corbies making moan, the one unto the other say, 'By yonder cliff we'll dine today.'	*Dum M. Stridulus solus* *ambulavit duos corvos audivit.* *Dixit quidam 'sub radice rupis* *hodie prandebimus.'*

19–22 January 2019

Part XXII: The voice of money

With seven weeks until *Brexit*, there's a frenzied search under way
for some workable means of retaining an *Irish* border
marked by no more than its signage, through which without any delay,
let or hindrance, traffic may pass in good order;
from *Dromore* to *DunLaoghaire*, to *Antrim* from *Drogheda*,
clear, open roads, free of toll booth and customs queue,
are to run north and south post-*Brexit* as now they do.

The *Backstop* must go, and the *Prime Minister*'s due in *Brussels*
with proposals (not yet disclosed) for what might take its place;
EU leaders, however, have been quietly flexing their muscles –
Will they cut her some slack? Will they give her some breathing space?
In public at least, they've shown hope a poker face;
Our agreement must stand, they maintain, *since its content defines*
thirty months of hard talking and fits with your own red lines.

Might there be movement in private? today's *Budgeriguardian*
says *Mrs May*'s on the heels of her elusive alternative prize;
it's a scheme close enough to her heart to be called *pericardian*
and, after its founder, the *Malthouse Compromise*;
once known as *Max-fac*, it facilitates and relies
on data transfer technology installed in a longer transition
using nanochips, lasers, and number-plate recognition.

Would it work? Some argue it's ready for installation
once leaders agree to give it the go-ahead;
for others, it's only the half-baked hallucination
of some *Europhobe* fantasist *Cuckooland* technohead.
And if *Malthouse* is *Max-fac* repackaged, as critics have said,
for all its allure, its persuasive traction is low;
Brussels looked at it back in the day, looked again, and said *No!*

Pipsqueak wonders in any case whether all this is just a decoy,
a proposal prepared for intentional misdirection;
suppose this technology talk were simply a ploy
to establish a discourse of compromise and rejection
while on the far rail a horse of a different complexion
made its way through the field, *Spiv* up, with a bagful of tricks
labelled *How much do you want?* or *Transactional Politics.*

It's worked once before, when the *Prime Minister* lifted the lid
off a treasure-chest funding ten votes from the *DUP*;
since it kept her in power, transferring a billion quid
from the taxpayer's pocket was as easy as *ABC*;
now *Vote Leave* constituencies backing a *Labour MP*
in the hard place between *Backstop* and a no-deal post-*Brexit* crash
might expect an injection of last-minute pre-*Brexit* cash.

All they'd need do would be vote for whatever plan
Mrs May put to the *Commons* having spoken with *President Tusk*;
there'd be no *Can* to carry, so no-one to carry the *Can*;
there'd be suppers to eat without anyone having to busk.
Bright sunshine would banish the coalfield community dusk,
transformative funds building hospitals, health centres, schools,
affordable homes, parks, gardens, bridges, roads, swimming pools.

Fools gold! declares *Lavery*; *Umunna* exclaims *It's a bung!*
Spreadsheet Phil, unperturbed, insists that it isn't a bribe;
Pipsqueak's thoughts lie uncollected and scattered among
a wild contraflow of endorsement and diatribe.
It's not *Pipsqueak*'s nature to let loose an undeserved gibe;
can someone persuade his hard head and soft heart to agree?
A voice in his ear whispers, *Pipsqueak, mirrez-vous y!*

Is it reason or conscience that offers such timely advice?
No matter – the point is how *Pipsqueak* himself would react
to the cynical premise that *Every bird has his price.*
What inducements would have him endorse a *Conservative* pact?
Quilted sandpaper? Handouts of fortified millet stacked
in waterproof outhouses all the way round his cage?
Net curtains? Blinds? Tinted mirrors? Short courses in *English Language*?

None of these, *Pipsqueak*'s sure, would exert gravitational force;
he'd raise two feathers to all, by way of expressing contempt;
Tory goose, *Tory* gander, could choke on their horseradish sauce
in the knowledge their effort was proven a futile attempt.
But would these small victories signify *Pipsqueak*'s exempt
from enticement, persuasion, surrender, conceding of ground,
or just that, so far, the right carrot had not been found?

So far, so clean-feathered. But suppose *Pipsqueak Elected Bird*
with constituent magpies, canaries, choughs, thrushes to represent,
suppose millet scarce, and all avian prospects deferred
through summers of drought and long winters of discontent;
might not some *Inducement* to *Pipsqueak* then seem heaven sent,
his own scruples be sandbagged to service a higher cause,
the well-being of others bought with the dirt on his claws?

Would he have the nerve, or the arrogance, to decline
the opening exchange of a grand transformational story
in which he throws his desperate birds a much-needed lifeline
and covers his shame with a fig-leaf, if not with glory?
All he need do's hold his nose, grit his beak, and vote *Tory*
but who knows if the bargain's too hard? what wise owl can say
whether *Paris* is worth that *Mass* at the end of the day?

So while *May* juggles *Malthouse*, do *Tory* chiefs calculate
the cost to buy off some *MPs* on the *Labour* side?
Ten million a seat – would that be sufficient bait,
or is it a case of *Multiply first, then divide*?
The *Impoverished Fourteen* might, given nowhere to hide,
be persuaded, this once, to become *Mrs May*'s voting friends
in return for a slice of her putative dividends.

Comes the day, comes the vote; tonight there's a warning bell
rung by *President Tusk* on the eve of *Mrs May*'s visit ;
he's been thinking about the particular place in *Hell*
kept for *Brexit Promoters* whose route maps were less than explicit.
His language is blunt and his timing is exquisite;
the *EU*'s united, the deal on the table is all,
here's a song about money, and which way the chips might fall:

A song

Money talks money talks that's no lie
you listen you hear you hear money sing
you listen you hear the till ring *ka-ching*
you spend it on everything
you spend it on anything
you spend it on bling
ka-ching ka-ching ka-ching
they say nothing money can't buy
cantus pecuniae
nothing money can't buy
that's a lie

yadda dadda
got to earn it to turn it
got to turn it to burn it
burn it the world goes round
Pipsqueak sleeps safe and sound
keep the pound keep the pound keep the pound
quid pro quo
pro quo's the way to go

no cash no money to burn so hard
no credit card life's hard
cold here on *Tuesday* night
cold here on *Saturday* night
cold here on *Brexit* night that's right
so cold on *Brexit* night

where's that hell place that hot place
you go when you die
you hide your face hide your face and you cry
that's no pie in the sky
money talks it's no lie
nothing money can't buy
that's a lie that's a lie.

4–7 February 2019

Part XXIII: Decision day's coming

For most of this month, *Pipsqueak*'s heard the dull clunk of a can
being kicked down the road by a dame in extravagant shoes;
the remorseless postponement of what must at last hit the fan
when the clock has run down and frantic *MPs* have to choose
between her deal and no deal, the twin options for *Brexit Blues*;
she's been dribbling her way to a last-minute, show-stopping thriller
giving *MPs* the perilous choice of *Charybdis* or *Scylla*.

Odysseus chose *Scylla*, the dangerous shoal of sharp rocks,
knowing perfectly well it must cost him six of his men;
May's deal would bring *Brexit* shrink-wrapped in a celluloid box,
though she'd risk losing support from her backstop-sick *DUP* ten.
But who'd risk *Charybdis*? No-deal is apocalypse when
a whirlpool engulfs us, dragging the whole ship down
through the fathomless, lung-bursting depths of the sea, and we drown.

The *Rees-Moggs* and the *Johnsons* are happy enough with no-deal;
they look straight in her eye and they do so with hardly a blink;
but less gung-ho palaverers cannot do other than squeal
with no life-belts to help, and no choice but to swim or to sink;
no-deal would leave *Pipsqueak* floundering in the drink
– not that *May*'s deal for him would be very much less of a pain;
he's a *Europhile Bird,* who still hopes against hope we'll remain.

Meanwhile, talks continue. In *Brussels,* the *PM*'s adviser
made some careless remarks in the bar of *La merle assoiffée*;
reporters nearby suddenly thought themselves somewhat wiser –
EU leaders, he said, had been rainchecking *Brexit Day*;
reports of his words only served to incense *Mrs May*
who dismissed them as gossip, the truth they expressed on a par
with '*what someone said someone said someone overheard in a bar.*'

She continues to market the terms of her *idée fixe*
while her ministers gripe and *Corbyn* drags *Labour*'s heels;
who do they think's fooled by their hamfisted confidence tricks
when the evidence shows the economy's losing its wheels?
When *Nissan* reneges on the *X-trail*, all *Sunderland* feels
the loss of substantial investment it thought it had won;
it's a blast of cold air from the *Land of the Rising Sun.*

There's worse news from *Honda*; the *Swindon* plant is to close;
at the end of two years, more than 3,000 jobs are to go.
Once again thanks to *Brexit* the *UK* economy slows,
and hard working people are dealt a life-damaging blow;
Pipsqueak paces his cage and asks what *Prime Ministers* know
of the angst ridden lives of the people they represent;
are there bailiffs in *Whitehall*? food banks in *Parliament?*

Pipsqueak's mirror can't show what *Decision Day* next month will bring
but today his keen eye catches hold of sensational stuff;
there's a prominent *Cambridge* postgraduate arguing
for *Remain* on terrestrial chat shows while sporting her buff;
to make argument clear, in black ink, between bosom and muff,
the words *Brexit leaves Britain naked* are aimed to disgruntle
any hard *Brexiteers* enjoying a glimpse of *Full Frontal.*

She's challenged *Rees-Mogg* to debate in his birthday suit
but *The Moggster*, if flattered, is not set to fall on his face;
his indignation is high, his sense of decorum acute –
he declines her kind thought with his usual unctuous grace.
Exhibitionist strategies clearly are out of place;
on a serious issue, the straightforward truth is enough;
if she'd spoken to *Pipsqueak* she might have been spared the rebuff.

Elsewhere *Pipsqueak*'s mirror discloses a threatening cloud
more substance than figment, more sinister than mirage;
it's a rowdy, malevolent, tricky-to-quantify crowd
of ex-*UKIP* defectors headed by *Nigel Farage*.
The new *Brexit Party*, in being but not yet at large,
declares itself ready for *EU* elections in *May*
should *Brexit* succumb by misfortune to any delay.

On *St Valentine's Day*, the *Conservatives* stage a rehearsal
for the meaningful vote that a fortnight hence should endorse
May's Brexit proposals, but this takes a wholesale reversal
when *Tory* abstentions blow her flotilla off course;
hard-line *Brexiteers* of both parties show no remorse;
Mrs May still determines to do her best with her plan
and once more with her right foot takes level aim at the can.

Imagine her foot, metatarsally streamlined, drawn back
in its *Russell and Bromley*, ready to make a strike
when just as she's poised to deliver a full-blooded whack
seven *Labour MPs* stride triumphantly up to the mic;
they've surrendered the whip, quit the party, so what's not to like?
She hesitates, halts, then with barely a downward glance
turns a might-have-been spot-kick into a tribal dance.

The *Magnificent Seven* next day are the *Magnificent Eight*
and *Watson* warns *Corbyn* of others preparing to leave;
he must show he's a genuine leader before it's too late
and stop keeping the cards that might win the game up his sleeve;
prospects of a general election only flatter him to deceive,
and it's actions, not words alone, that must silence the critic
who says that the party is, to its shame, anti-*Semitic*.

Two days later, three *Tories* declare themselves *Independent*;
defectors from both sides are shifting to centre ground;
the media ask if new currents are in the ascendant
and whether or not their impact will be profound;
Mrs May's off to *Egypt* but can she sleep safe and sound
while her ministers back at home state publicly (it's no lie)
she should step down in three months, *leaving Number 10 'on a high'*?

It's time to delay, time to launch that poke at the can;
the meaningful vote planned for this week will not now take place
let *Gove*, *Rudd* and *Johnson* feel the heat in their frying pan,
Hunt, *Javid* and *Raab* vainly canvas a power base.
EU leaders in *Sharm* declare *March 12th* a disgrace;
Prime Minister Rutte says we're *sleepwalking towards no deal*;
alarm bells are ringing; *it's time to wake up and get real.*

From the depths of the desert, the *EU* have conjured a rabbit,
an undersized creature that's utterly dwarfed by the hat
into which they have bundled it so they can practise the habit
of partial disclosure, their encore to *Schrödinger's Cat*;
they don't do *Hey Prestoes,* they don't do shouts of *Howzat!*
They just proffer the headgear, its interior covered by lint,
give a quick glimpse of fur, and hope *Mrs May* takes the hint.

It takes two to tango, says *Juncker, and I know how to dance*;
there's something on offer a few steps away down the road;
does *May* have the gumption to recognise there's a chance
of some *EU* concession-in-waiting wrapped up in that code?
Time to proffer the hat in which the rabbit's been stowed;
time for *President Tusk* to make his distinct contribution;
Pushing Brexit Day back would be a rational solution.

It's the end of the month, and *Mrs May*'s flown back from *Sharm*
having listened, perhaps, to whatever the *EU* has said;
a *Commons* announcement sounds an unwelcome alarm
to anyone thinking prospects of remain are stone dead;
if *her plan* on *12th* takes a meaningful knock on the head,
there'll be a yes-or-no vote on *no-deal* put the following day,
and if that's lost, on *14th*, a meaningful vote on *delay*.

Pipsqueak is encouraged, the more so since *Labour,* at last,
with their own *Brexit* proposals forfeiting *Commons* support,
back a new referendum, intending the verdict be passed
to the *British Electorate*, jury of last resort.
There's many a slip, and many a pothole to thwart
Pipsqueak's hopes of remain, but now there's the slenderest chance
that our sleepwalk will end, and the *UK* will wake from its trance.

A song

Hopscotch! Hopscotch! *Ascoliasmus luditur!*
That's what we gonna play!
We gonna play hopscotch, hopscotch,
We gonna tell Mrs May *Ascoliasmim Theresam*
We don't want her Brexit deal,
We don't want Brexit, we wanna stay! *Docebimus ut Brexitum nolemus!*

Mark a Yes and a No on the floor of the house
For the first day of play;
Put a Y for a Yes, that's a why? oh why? oh why?
Put an N for a No, be sure that's the way to go.

When she asks on Day 1, *Ante diem IV Id. Mar.*
Do you want my Brexit plan?
Go straight to that No, tell her, No, no way, man!
No, no, no, no, we don't want your plan!
Not your Brexit plan, not your Brexit plan, no way, man!
Brexitum tuum nullo modo volemus!

Hopscotch! Hopscotch!
That's what we gonna play!
We gonna play hopscotch, hopscotch,
We gonna tell Mrs May
We don't want her Brexit deal,
We don't want Brexit, we wanna stay!

Mark a Yes and a No on the floor of the house
For the second day of play;
Put a Y for a Yes, that's a why? oh why? oh why?
Put an N for a No, be sure that's the way to go.

When she asks on Day 2, *Ante diem III Id. Mar.*
Do you want Brexit no deal?
Go straight to that No and tell her,
No way, Mrs May,
Get real, get real! *Nullo modo, mehecule!*
No deal makes me squeal, that's how I feel, *Veritatem respice!*
Not Brexit no deal, not no deal, that's my answer, get real!

Hopscotch! Hopscotch!
That's what we gonna play!
We gonna play hopscotch, hopscotch,
We gonna tell Mrs May
We don't want a no deal Brexit,
We don't want Brexit, we wanna stay!

Mark a Yes and a No on the floor of the house
For the third day of play;
Put an N for a No, today that's no way to go,
Put a Y for a Yes, how did you guess?
Yes, Yes , Yes, that's a Yes.

When she asks on Day 3, *Pridie Id. Mar.*
Do you want to delay? *Imo dicetur!*
Progress to that Yes and say,
How did you guess, Mrs May?
Yes, Yes, Yes, Couldn't you guess, Mrs May?
Yes, yes, yes, yes *Imo! Imo! Imo!*
Delay's what we say, save the day with delay, *Procrastinare*
That's the way, Mrs May. *volemus non conjicere potuisti?*

Hopscotch! Hopscotch!
That's what we gonna play!
We gonna play hopscotch, hopscotch,
We gonna tell Mrs May
We don't want her Brexit deal,
We don't want Brexit, we wanna stay!

If we get a delay
There's one more choice of which way,
A choice of we go or we stay;
That's the choice, Mrs May
And when it comes to the choice we say
No, No, No to we go
We say Yes to we stay, and we stay.

Et postea?

in referendo secundo

manere tenebimus.

27 February–5 March 2019

Part XXIV: Countdown and beyond

We've walked all the way to the edge of a perilous cliff
but the *Prime Minister*'s plan's had two meaningful knocks on the head
and no-deal for the moment's exuding a moribund whiff
since the *Commons* by four votes decided they'd leave it for dead.
The *Government*'s lost any claim it once had to street cred
now the *Speaker*'s disrupted *Mrs May*'s precious *Brexit Planner*
with a large, unexpected, unwelcome *Procedural Spanner*.

His archives reveal that since the year before *Gunpowder Plot*
once the *Commons* have voted down a particular motion
the convention has been that identical proposals may not
be presented again, nor may any *similar* notion.
He's therefore declared, amid *Tory Party* commotion,
that with two plans rejected, if *Mrs May* proffers a third,
it must be *substantially different*, if it is to be heard.

It gave her two days before the next *EU/UK* summit
at which she must ask for a longer or shorter delay;
she'd been told that her hopes for a *Brexit* extension would plummet
if the *EU* weren't convinced she had something new to say.
In under ten days we were due to hit *Brexit Day*;
so something was needed to make old proposals look new
and a sufficient extension in order to squeeze *Brexit* through.

She was after three months, but the *EU* elections take place
in the last week of *May*, so the last day of *June*'s a non-starter;
it remains to be seen whether *Everything that is the Case*
has a small ad appear in the *Tory Exchange and Martyr*
reading *Wanted – replacement Prime Minister. Willing to barter.*
Backstage, talks continued with *Lucas*, *Sturgeon*, *Cable*, and *Dodds*
in search of support, albeit against the odds.

Not with *Corbyn* however, who, finding *Umunna* invited,
turned round on his heel and strode out of the room in a huff,
his distrust of a turncoat so strong that he felt himself slighted
(could he not just this once have taken the smooth with the rough?)
The *Prime Minister's* broadcast later that night was the stuff
self-delusion is made of, laying blame on the other side
and assuring the public *I'm with you. I'm on your side.*

Pipsqueak knows that she's not. A petition set up to *Revoke*
Article 50 so far has secured more than 5,000,000 names
and while she's quite prepared to see *Britain* go up in smoke
there are 1,000,000 people marching to quench the flames.
She was right to maintain that a *Government* plays no games,
but nor do the public, whose lives tell a commonplace story
of hard work and endeavour, even some of those voting *Tory*.

The *EU* at its summit agreed the *UK* can remain
until *April 12th*, and beyond if it can *indicate*
a way forward, and at the same time *undertake to campaign*
in the EU elections. So in three further weeks of debate
we must chart a fresh course for our *Brexit*-bound ship of state,
make the best use we can of an unearned last-minute reprieve,
turn away from the rocks and rethink our decision to leave.

The *Commons*, two days ago, voted to set aside
time later this week to take some indicative votes
on alternative strategies, making a bid to decide
which one they prefer, or at least does not stick in their throats.
But just as they're starting to sort out the sheep from the goats
the *Prime Minister's* dice are given one last, desperate throw;
Get Brexit in place, she tells *Tory MPs*, *and I'll go.*

What occurs at the surface reflects what has happened beneath,
the shifts in the bedrock, the currents that come into play,
and as voting goes on, there's an audible gritting of teeth
as once bitter opponents inch closer to *Mrs May*;
crafty *Bullingdon Boris* declared only yesterday
that *Mrs May's* plan would impale the *UK* on a skewer;
today opportunity knocks and his scruples are fewer.

The *Commons* have spoken, and all eight amendments are lost;
a democrat nation reels crazily over the edge;
next week must decide whether *Mrs May*'s lines can be crossed
by a salvaged amendment, the thin end of sanity's wedge.
The *Bowler Hats* have announced that, notwithstanding her pledge,
though *Mrs May*'s deal reappear, and the *Speaker* allow it,
while the backstop's in place they'll continue to disavow it.

Pipsqueak's cheered by the portents; *All Fool's Day* has not yet arrived
but the balance is shifting, the deck has been rearranged;
among possible outcomes, a fresh *People's Vote* has survived,
giving hope in the end that no-one will be short-changed.
The contempt of the bigot, the zeal of the frankly deranged
may yet come to nothing, delusional strategies fail,
Faction find herself homeless, and at the last *Wisdom* prevail.

30 March

It's been *Pipsqueak*'s intention, devising these vehement squibs,
to reprove and admonish, to document and record,
taking aim at the heart, at the head, at the belly, the ribs,
to repudiate folly, and where merit's earned, to reward;
when folly runs riot and rational judgement's obscured,
Pipsqueak's there at your side, outpouring his disaffection,
a critical friend recommending a change of direction.

31 March

We've twelve days of remission (not exactly of borrowed time)
then for lack of agreement, we'll quit the *EU* with no deal;
internal dissension has left us with mountains to climb
and vindictive dislikes we're now scarcely at pains to conceal;
we must somehow cool hatreds and give our wounds time to heal,
find common cause with our neighbour, break through the armoured glass
with which each walls his thinking, and so end the *Brexit impasse*.

It's forty-eight hours since *Mrs May*'s plan was rejected
at the third time of asking, and anger broke out in the streets;
Brexiteers who were irked at a referendum result disrespected
found themselves once again on the sharp end of successive defeats;
Remainers know well how corrosive frustration eats
at the heart, at the liver, the kidneys, the roots of the hair;
objectives may differ but this much at least we share.

It's said that the prospect of being hanged in the morning
gives focus to purpose and steadies a wavering mind;
will the prospect of no deal give *MPs* a similar warning
and lead them towards what so far they're unable to find?
Pipsqueak fervently hopes to see policy redefined,
tomorrow's indicative votes mark an end to obstruction,
and advice to the government quickly become an instruction.

1 April

But when push comes to shove, what *Pipsqueak* hopes isn't to be;
Commons factions prevail, and no motion can win their support.
Has no more emerged than agreement to disagree?
Is *Pipsqueak*'s *No Brexit* no more than delusional thought?
The figures reveal by what margin each motion falls short;
round a narrow defeat fresh thinking may yet coalesce
and at this late hour revive *Pipsqueak*'s faint hope of success.

A margin of only three votes went against *Zollverein*
and eight was the margin by which a *Public Vote* fell;
the arithmetic shows that such verdicts are borderline
like the one three years back that still holds us entrapped in its spell;
such slender majorities ring true democracy's knell
when a handful determines what a whole nation must do
and the will of the people at root is the will of the few.

There are rumours tonight that *Mrs May* plans to bring
her *Withdrawal Agreement* back a fourth time for a vote;
if she does, it's not certain sufficient *MPs* will sing
from the hymn sheet provided, or even hit the same note;
it's her sheer brass persistence that lacerates *Pipsqueak*'s throat,
the relentless pursuit of a deeply flawed proposition
driven not by persuasion, but by the blind force of attrition.

2 April

It's come back once again, and by an unusual route
the *Prime Minister* wants to engage *Jeremy Corbyn* in talks;
it remains to be seen if this last-minute gesture bears fruit,
if a compromise takes up its dirty bed-linen and walks.
Can what appeals to the doves ever truly placate the hawks?
What future for *Pipsqueak* and all those whom *Brexit* offends
should disputes over means be resolved in the interest of ends?

3–5 April

By one vote, the *Commons* mandate *Mrs May* to apply
for a further deferral, which *Pipsqueak* suspects may be long;
not that she for one moment has come over *Brexit* shy
but that *Brussels* believes any more short delays would be wrong.
And it might be no more than seven days now till the gong
sends *Mrs May* packing with no chance of further appeal,
and consigns the *UK* to the barren wastes of no deal.

Is the *Prime Minister* clever? Or is she merely obtuse?
Her request, made today, is once more for the last day of *June*;
to decline it, the *EU* will need precious little excuse;
Mrs May would be better advised if she asked for the *Moon*.
There's not very much that makes *Mrs May* change her tune;
given *No* for an answer she'll look over her shoulder and then
she'll ask the same question again, and again, and again.

Or is this a manoeuvre, the outcome of which is expected
to be a refusal, to show that at least she tried,
when, as she knows it must be, her application's rejected,
and she'll be under pressure to keep hard *Brexiteers* onside?
Time's running out fast but supposing the *EU* decide
on what *President Tusk* calls an up-to-a-twelvemonth *flextension*,
would that be enough time to settle our bone of contention?

6 April

It's *Grand National Day*, and *Pipsqueak* has squandered a bag
of his fortified millet at odds of a hundred to one
on a plodding, short-winded, lame, halting, recalcitrant nag
whose chance at the off barely came before it was gone;
he'd have done a lot better to stake his inheritance on
some thoroughbred *Pegasus* able to win at a stroll
such as *Anibale Fly*, *Rathvinden*, or *Tiger Roll*.

Will the *Brexit Day Handicap* yield him a better result?
The going is muddy, and no-one's yet mapped out the course.
The betting is slack; there are no decent odds to consult;
few punters back *Corbyn* or *May* when astride of that horse.
Pipsqueak at the finish is sure to be full of remorse
if the fateful day comes, marked more by rain than by shine,
when, whoever is up, *Brexit* stumbles across the line.

It still may not happen. There's still no agreement in sight
between *Corbyn* and *May*, who's reluctant to compromise,
but there's just about time for the *Commons* to see the light
and put forward a plan for *Brussels* to scrutinise;
to win time for *Remain*, we must surely agree to revise
all thought of red lines, and propose, for the good of the nation,
a fresh *People's Vote*, fresh thinking, a fresh conversation.

7–9 April

How many birds beside *Pipsqueak* would welcome a long delay?
It would give time for reflection, stocktaking, and dialogue;
it would mean taking part in the *EU* elections in *May*
to the chagrin of *Leadsom*, the niggle and chafe of *Rees-Mogg*.
With *Brussels*' assistance we might find a path through the fog,
though the *Moggster* declares *UK* strategy, round the clock,
should consist of three elements – *Veto, Obstruct,* and *Block*.

Can *Mrs May* have any appetite left to engage
now so much has been lost and there's still so little to show?
How many days can be left before she herself quits the stage
or malcontent *Tories,* grown savage, compel her to go?
In a week or a month she'll be gone and *Pipsqueak* will know
which *Europhobe Minister*, roughshod and eager to climb,
uncloset*s Ambition*, steps out, and succeeds her as *Prime*.

Leaving *Tory* and *Labour* to talk on *through gritted teeth*,
she's flown to *Berlin* and to *Paris* ahead of the *Summit*;
on the surface, it's smiles, but those worry lines underneath
show anxiety's there and she's powerless to overcome it.
However it goes, her credit with *Tories* must plummet;
while the six weeks she wants mean that *Tory* impatience lingers
any longer delay *risks letting Brexit slip through our fingers*.

10–12 April

The *EU* has declined to let *Mrs May* off the hook
and the prospects for *Brexit* are luckily still problematical;
Pipsqueak's polychrome verses are soon to be bound in a book
and the time's close at hand for *Yours Truly* to take a sabbatical;
the moment has come for *Pipsqueak* to turn wholly pragmatical
and suspend his discourse on the seen and the unforeseen,
the fortunes of *Brexit* from *April* to *Hallowe'en.*

In the *EU* elections he wants us to nominate
creative *Remainers*, not those bent on sabotage;
good will and good manners are what's required to frustrate
the disruptive designs of *Rees-Mogg* and his entourage.
We've seen far too much of loudmouths like *Nigel Farage*;
the *UK*'s representatives need to be socially skilled,
bridge-building *Europhiles*, ready and willing to build.

There's time for a *People's Vote*, time for a *General Election*,
time to jettison folly, take soundings and steady the ship;
we can redeem our mistakes with a radical change of direction
if we butter our fingers, unlock, and let *Brexit* slip;
there's time too for hard *Brexit* to work up a stranglehold grip
should *Leadsom, Fox, Raab, Davis, Duncan Smith* have their way
and *Bullingdon Boris* by *June* have replaced *Mrs May.*

A day's coming next month which *Pipsqueak* anticipates
with unrestrained pleasure, excitement and gratitude;
it's a festive occasion he annually celebrates
with music and dancing, red ribbons, spectacular food;
it's a day when new friendships are made and old friendships renewed;
it's joyful, gregarious, a day for the meeting of minds,
the last before *Pipsqueak* reluctantly draws down his blinds.

One day in May

It's springtime once more, and time for a *reverdie*
in praise of sap rising, of *April*'s beneficent showers,
the catkins-burst hedgerows bright with fresh greenery,
the music of insects that joyfully plunder the flowers;
a sense of resurgence invigorates *Pipsqueak Towers*,
its impulse, the date – it's *Thursday 9 May*,
warm, sunny, and dry, as always on *Pipsqueak*'s birthday.

How old the bird is, this is no place to disclose;
he's as old as his tongue and precisely as old as his beak,
old enough to know better than bottle up all his woes,
pipe down on his perch and start turning the other cheek.
There's little enough whereof *Stridulus* cannot speak
but today's not for satire; just swing by his cage and partake
of choice cuttlefish cubes, fresh millet and birthday cake.

The bars of his cage are glinting like beams of the sun,
his mirror is polished, his floor has been sandpapered flat;
his fountains run clear, his housekeeping chores are all done,
there's a rosette on his perch, a scatter of cards on his mat.
He opens them, scans them, rejoices; then, all of a sudden, *What's that?*
a brown *C9 Envelope*, franked, and to his consternation
there's a summons inside from *Home Office Immigration*.

It claims he's an *Alien Bird* with no legal right of abode
in a country reclaiming control of its national borders;
he'd best quit his perch, pack his bags, and take to the road
before *Tory* intransigence gives him his marching orders.
There's no place in *Britain* for aliens, migrants, defrauders
(the *Commons* excepted); all elsewhere are brought to book;
il faut foutre le camp, and *Pipsqueak* must sling his hook.

The Centre requires him to appear by the end of next week
and accept deportation or otherwise fight his case;
he should bring his entitlements, and may bring others to speak
for him at the said time and in the appointed place;
the *Crown's Agent* and *Pipsqueak* will hammer out face to face
(each has strong arguments, each has an agile brain)
whether *Pipsqueak* must leave or if he's allowed to remain.

But his guests are invited, the party must go ahead;
Pipsqueak's terrace is heaving already with starling and thrush;
flocks of sparrows are foraging nibbles from stale crusts of bread,
chough, magpie and gannet descend on his mulberry bush;
the owl and the cuckoo stand somewhat apart from the crush
rehearsing their parts, as professional choristers do,
for when the time comes to sing *Happy Birthday to You.*

It's a boisterous throng, with which *Pipsqueak* is glad to mingle;
the chaffer and *craic* afford pleasure that's unconfined;
as the party goes on the polyglot buzz brings a tingle
of joy and excitement, a rapturous thrill to the mind.
Now the chorus is ringing, but *Pipsqueak* can't wholly unwind;
though mirth mark the owl's and glee mark the cuckoo's note,
it's sorrow, not happiness, raises a lump in his throat.

Alienation's a choke-pear that aggravates *Pipsqueak*'s gorge;
he's a hard-working, patriot bird and he's done no wrong.
His concern all these years has been to bring to his forge
the discontents of the age, and hammer them into song.
In response to the question, *Where is it that you belong?*
the satirist's answer must always ring loud and clear,
If you're vexed by your face in my mirror, I must belong here.

All too soon, it's the moment to set about slicing the cake;
all too soon, it's devoured, and *Jenny Wren*'s hunting for crumbs;
one by one the birds fly, and *Pipsqueak*'s alone with the ache
of his thoughts, apprehensions, the loneliness that benumbs.
Who's there to support him, speak up for him now the crunch comes?
Experience tells him how most of these summonses end
and *Pipsqueak* right now is in desperate need of a friend.

* * * *

At the end of the terrace his mulberry bush is astir;
there's a bright flash of gold, azure shoulder and ebony claw;
the overcast afternoon sky erupts in a blur
as out from the bush flies a fire-breathing *Blue Macaw*;
he circles, swoops, hovers, alighting at *Pipsqueak*'s door.
With *Salve, amice!* he opens his liquorice beak
and to *Pipsqueak*'s astonishment asks for permission to speak.

'*By all means*,' declares *Pipsqueak*, '*but tell me to what do I owe...?*'
The *Macaw* interrupts, '*Peace, cousin; attend to the word
of Polychrome Parrot, who five hundred years ago
was Papagay Peerless, Dan Skelton's satirical bird;
we stripped the mask off hypocrisy, ridiculed the absurd,
exposed government folly, taught selfishness charity,
and awoke what was decent in erring humanity.*

*From the bowge of your beak it is plain we are kith and kin
and the values you hold are the very same values I share;
Peerless Parrot and Pipsqueak, fellow satirists under the skin,
serve equality, justice, compassion and truth everywhere;
let obstinate bigots and self-serving politicians beware
when Papagay Peerless confronts them with what is right
or Pipsqueak the Brave holds their shameful deeds to the light.*

'Though your Latin limps lamely and it's clear you have little Greek
to grace versemaking with, your own native language suffices;
plain words deliver plain truth when you open your beak
and classical rhetoric's left to her own devices;
your sturdy vernacular needs no anagnorises,
no Stagirite apophthegms lending you spurious weight;
indignation's authentic when poetry tells it straight.

'We are quarrelsome reprobates, blessed with the power of speech,
two poets, two patriots watching our country bleed;
rest assured our joint strength more than doubles the power of each
and I've come to stand by my friend in his hour of most need.
At the end of next week, side by side you and I will proceed
to this Home Office hearing, where we'll demonstrate none can gainsay
either Pipsqueak the Brave or his nonpareil Papagay.

'And don't think we're alone; Master Skelton himself's on the road,
his thirst still unquenched after drinking from Helicon's well;
his spirit stands by us, impatient to shoulder its load,
and pack time-serving Home Office Jobsworths off squealing to Hell;
pseudo-patriot chisellers have a peculiar smell
– cologne-scented horseshit combined with the odour of bear;
we three will dispel it with furious blasts of fresh air.

'Best of all, there is Smokestack, the midwife to Pipsqueak's complaints;
he's collected your verses and gathered them into a book;
and whoever examines the picture that Squeak, Budgie! paints
will have no more truck with political gobbledegook;
they'll come forward in droves to get Pipsqueak the Brave off the hook
and their children, years later, will turn to its pages in search
of the truths and the home truths delivered from Pipsqueak's perch.'

* * * *

How the matter's resolved must at this point be left in suspense;
Pipsqueak's fate is on hold for the critical reader to judge.
Will his purging our discontents be sufficient defence
against *Tory* malevolence nursing an avian grudge?
Or will rank *Xenophobia* join with *Injustice* to nudge
our friend from the perch which he's occupied for so long
pitching him out on his ear with *Good riddance! You don't belong?*

We are where we are, in an unstable, uncertain position,
vindictive and quarrelsome, overwrought, lacking composure;
will another six months see us locked in post-*Brexit* transition
our febrile antipathies stirred by continued exposure?
Or shall we attain some less barbarous version of closure,
a skein, a rapport we continue to share with our friends
imperfect of course, but woven from these loose ends?

The time has now come to pull down the blackout blind,
let the dustsheet of darkness bring silence to *Pipsqueak*'s cage;
what we think of as endings are only beginnings consigned
to the talents and care of a later, more scrupulous, age;
let *Parrot* and *Pipsqueak*, our two critical cousins, engage
in a song of departure, an anthem for psittacine voices
called *Are we on our way out?* or *We have to live with our choices.*

A duet sung by Pipsqueak and Papagay

The endgame's upon us;
        (Magistri terrae sumus)
the winners think themselves peacocks
        (sese quasi deos credunt)
and then suddenly – checkmate!
        (et subito! nasi in pulvere)
we're dead ducks after all.
        (quid sumus? verminosi.)

The vultures are flying
        (et super nos aves)
over our chequered board;
        (qui nos minusculos vident)
how tiny we seem to them!
        (volvunt, volvunt super nos)
You're crazy! You're crazy! they cry.
        (et insani! insani! clamant.)

We're swanning around in our folly;
        (omnes in moriis natamus)
we make flags for ourselves,
        (vexillas inveniemus)
sew badges onto our shirts;
        (super indusia insignia pandimus)
underneath, we're just people.
        (sub indusiis ossa pellisque sumus)

The world has gone crazy.
        (audite mundum insanum)
Give us death! we shout, *Give us endgames!*
        (vivat mors! vivat terminus!)
No-one shouts *Give us life!*
        (nemo vivat vita! clamat)
We're assassins, the lot of us.
        (omnes percussores sumus)

The whole earth is groaning;
(et omnis terra gemiscens)
it's a great time for eruptions;
(tempestivitas volcanos)
we'll turn the world upside down.
(mundum confundere imus)
Hold tight! All the chessmen are falling!
(constringete pugnis, omnia fugunt!)

And the vultures above us
(et super nos aves)
in whose eyes we seem so tiny
(qui nos minusculos vident)
fly round in their crazy circles
(volvunt quasi insani)
shrieking *It's checkmate*! *You're ours! You're ours!*
(et nostri! nostri! clamant.)

How beautiful life could be
(vita quam dulcis esset)
if only we learned to live it!
(si primum vivere volumus)
Why should we cudgel our brains
(cur cerebrum frangere)
when there's bright sunshine outside?
(dum foris lucet formosus sol?)

With so many beautiful people
(et enim sunt populi pulchri)
and glorious sunshine outside
(et foris lucet formosus sol)
why drive ourselves frantic?
(cur cerebrum frangere?)
To hell with all that! Let's learn to live!
(ad Avernos omnia! primum vivamus!)

The endgame's upon us;
(magistri terrae sumus)
the winners think themselves peacocks;
(sese quasi deos credunt)
and the vultures above us cry
(et super nos clamant aves)
They're crazy! they're crazy! They're ours!
(*insani! insani! sunt nostri!*)

Envoi

Place the cloth on *Pipsqueak*'s palace
marred with moth holes and frayed ends;
wholly without scorn or malice
Pipsqueak to his foes extends
these bitter draughts from satire's chalice,
these crumbs of comfort to his friends.

Acknowledgements

Versions of most of these poems have been posted on *Facebook* as they have been completed. An extract from part IV appeared in *Stand* Volume 15 (4) 216/2017.